The Christian Communicator's Handbook

The Christian
Communicator's
Handbook

Dr. Tom Nash

VICTOR BOOKS

A DIVISION OF SCRIPTURE PRESS PUBLICATIONS INC.
USA CANADA ENGLAND

Unless otherwise noted, Scripture quotations are from the *Holy Bible,
New International Version®*. Copyright © 1973, 1978, 1984 by
International Bible Society. Used by permission of
Zondervan Publishing House. All rights reserved.
Quotations marked NASB are from the *New American Standard Bible,*
© the Lockman Foundation 1960, 1962, 1963, 1968, 1971, 1972,
1973, 1975, 1977. Quotations marked KJV are from
the *Authorized (King James) Version.*

Cover Design: Scott Rattray

Library of Congress Cataloging-in-Publication Data

Nash, Tom, Dr.
  The Christian communicator's handbook / by Tom Nash.
     p.   cm.
  Includes bibliographical references.
  ISBN: 1-56476-384-6
  1. Communication—Religious aspects—Christianity.
  2. Evangelistic work.   I. Title.
  BV4319.N36   1995
  269'.2'014—dc20   94-34681
                                                          CIP

---

1 2 3 4 5 6 7 8 9 10   Printing/Year   99 98 97 96 95

Contents

to Sylvia

How to Make This Book Work for You

You can become a more effective communicator. *Nothing* is more important.

Outrageous? Think about this: without food and water you would die, but without communication life would have no meaning anyway. If God had not communicated with us, we would have no purpose in life and no hope for a life to come.

We spend most of our time sending and receiving messages. In past centuries people spent much of their time doing physical labor, but now most of us work by communicating. We accomplish our tasks mostly by using words and symbols instead of physically manipulating objects.

Think of all the really important things that depend on communication. You can't win a convert, or a wife, without communicating. We know the Lord only because He communicated with us. Even our worship is a form of communication.

How good are you at communicating? Is there room for improvement?

That's not a fair question.

Unless you are in a situation where you regularly get accurate feedback, you don't know how well you communicate. As a college professor, I sometimes think I explain a concept brilliantly. Then I give a quiz and find that most of the students don't "get it." Reality sets in.

Most of us are aware our communication isn't perfect. We blow it big-time often enough to realize we have room for change. How much could you improve? Most people could easily double their effectiveness by putting the ideas in this book into practice. Some could become 10 times or even 100 times more effective.

What would it be like if *you* were a better communicator?

Imagine! People would be more interested in what you say. They would understand you better. More lives could be changed. Your family life would be enriched. You would have fewer disagreements. Your prayer life would improve. You might even earn more.

You can greatly increase your effectiveness by using simple communication principles, most of which are found in the Bible. But there is a catch. You must first understand the principles, then habitually apply them to your life. That's what this book will help you do.

The Bible and Science

I have been studying both the Bible and scientific communication theory for many years and have come to a startling conclusion: they agree. If the Bible is true and if science (though often misused) is a search for truth, they should arrive at the same point. They often do! All truth is God's truth.

While the Bible is not organized as a communication text, it is still a very useful source on the subject. By noticing how God communicates, we can greatly improve our communication.

Recent scientific findings are also very helpful. Especially since World War II, researchers have conducted thousands of communication studies. By trial and error they have uncovered a vast amount of useful information about what works and what doesn't. I have tried to glean the most useful findings for you.

How to Make This Book Work for You

You can use this book in several ways.

- Read it all to gain a good overview of ways to improve communication. The book is organized logically to give you a complete picture of the communication process. Because you will tend to forget what you read, underline useful passages, "dog ear" important pages, and write notes to yourself in the margins and inside covers.

- Skim it by reading the boldfaced summary statements. Read these like proverbs — to find what is *generally* true. They are too succinct to include all the qualifications and exceptions.

- Use it to solve specific problems. Perhaps you have experienced a recent "failure to communicate." Or maybe you just took on some new responsibility, and you're not sure how to approach it. Use the table of contents to guide you to sections that are especially pertinent to your immediate needs.

- Use it as a text for a class or the basis for a more in-depth study. The notes at the end of each chapter offer recommendations for more study and additional sources.

Who Should Use This Book

I designed this book to be especially useful to Christians who wish to increase their effectiveness in life and ministry. I address common problems we all face.

While writing I was thinking of the needs of pastors, elders, Sunday School teachers, youth leaders, home Bible study teachers, school teachers, administrators, counselors, Christian broadcasters, bookstore personnel, camp directors, parents, spouses, and many others who need and want to improve their skills.

Communicating Christianly

With knowledge comes power, with power, responsibility.

Much of the communication we experience every day, sometimes even from Christian sources, involves techniques that are not of God. We are so immersed in the culture of this world that we may adopt its methods uncritically. Ungodly lifestyles begin to seem normal. Lying seems OK. Adultery? No problem.

Exaggeration, half-truths, and deception all have their source in the father of lies. Jesus did not pressure people into believing. He clearly presented truth and respected people's choices. He let the rich young ruler walk away.

Communicating well requires our best thinking, creativity, imagination, knowledge, and plenty of hard work. It will also require careful thought as to the ethics of how we use these powerful tools. I have pointed out some possible traps and labeled them, **Ethical Point.** Please give these statements careful thought.

Hearing and Doing

Knowing how to be a better communicator is a start, but unless you change what you *do* there is no profit. I have tried to present the ideas in this book in a practical way so you can easily do them. The book will be vastly more beneficial if you actually take the time to practice the ideas.

When you come across an idea that would work in your life, stop and think of a specific situation in which you could apply it. Plan out the very words you might say. If possible, rehearse them out loud. Then, "just do it."

Expect to forget. By the time you finish reading a chapter, you will have already forgotten most of the points at the beginning. So, when you find a good idea, mark it, then periodically go back and reread it.

The Lord bless you as you make a significant difference in your life and the lives of others by improving your communication skills. It really will change your life.

Gather Information

CHAPTER ONE

Learn to Listen

Want to be a great communicator? Learn to listen!
Information reception skills are key to both sides of
communication, receiving and giving. All of us spend
more time receiving than sending messages, but we can also
become better senders through becoming better receivers. How?

- Learning about the reception process can help you design messages that can be better understood.

- Becoming a better receiver will help you understand those with whom you communicate so your messages can be more on target.

While this chapter primarily addresses listening, most of the
points are equally valid for reading or other forms of information reception.

Failures to Listen

See if you can identify with any of these failures to communicate.

Situation One

Frank and Mary are having an animated conversation in a restaurant. Each can hardly wait for an opening to get the next point across. In fact, they often interrupt each other. The problem is, both are so busy thinking of their next statement they don't really *listen* to each other. This isn't a dialogue, but merely two monologues intertwined. Each speaks with sincere feeling and intensity, but little *communication* takes place.

Situation Two

Boyfriend to girlfriend on college campus: "I'll meet you after class in front of the library."
Girlfriend: "See ya."
Later that evening, girlfriend, furious: "Where *were* you! I waited more than an hour, and I missed lunch."
Boyfriend: "Where was *I*? I was at the library like I said. Where were *you*?
Girlfriend: "You couldn't have been. I was there the whole time."
Boyfriend: "So was I."

(beat)

Girlfriend: "*Where* at the library were you?"
Boyfriend: "Right in front, like I said. Across from Metzger Hall."
Girlfriend: "That's not the front. The front is across from the medical center."

Situation Three

Harry, who is not a Christian, is commuting home. He gets tired of his usual radio station, so he hits "search." He hears bits of several different kinds of music and talk shows including a few words from a sermon. It seems to have no relevance to him, so he continues to "search."

16

Situation Four

You're sitting in class (or church, etc.), and the teacher (leader, pastor, professor) is taking too long to make his point. You start thinking about something else, perhaps some pressing matter you have to take care of. Your thoughts wander for a few minutes.

A bit later the speaker changes his voice slightly or makes a pause, so you check in again with the lesson. But before long you drift away again. The next time you check in the lesson doesn't make sense. You've apparently missed some critical point. Oh well. You give up and spend the rest of the time thinking about other things, or doodling, or squirming. The lesson was a total loss.

Whose fault were these failures to communicate? Consider these three theories.

Figure out *what* went wrong, not *who* was wrong when communication breaks down.

- It was the speaker's fault. He/she should have found ways to hold the listener's attention and communicate clearly.

- It was the listener's fault. The listener should pay attention and understand correctly.

- It's not very helpful to assign fault because you can only directly control one side of the communication process at a time. To be an effective communicator you need to be the best sender and receiver you can be. Some people you need to hear will not be skillful communicators, so you will need to learn to listen well. Some people who need to

17

hear you aren't very good listeners, so you will need to be a skillful sender. You can't entirely make up for the deficiencies on the other side, but you can learn skills that will greatly help the communication process.

Reasons to Listen

Before we explore ways to become more effective listeners, we need to think about *why* we listen. Sometimes we overhear by accident, with no real intention of listening. We hear others' conversations at restaurants, parties, and offices. We tolerate commercials and other material to hear what we tuned in for. We hear boom boxes at beaches, loud car radios, and all sorts of noises through thin apartment walls.

Most of our listening is done on purpose. We listen:

- to pass time, reduce boredom;
- for entertainment, to experience pleasant emotions;
- to escape mentally from pressing problems, fears, and tensions;
- for mood control (cheer up, calm down);
- for companionship;
- because we are required or expected to do so;
- to please another person, whom we admire;
- to receive information to pass on to others, to avoid appearing ignorant or to maintain a position of opinion leadership; (A male friend and I were going to the mountains to do some skeet shooting. First he wanted to watch enough of a football game so he could witness one significant play which he could mention to his colleagues at work the next day. My friend was not a football fan, but didn't want to appear ignorant.)
- to evaluate the speaker and/or message; and

- to find information we need or might need to solve present or future problems.

We can see from all of this that listeners have their own reasons for listening. These reasons may be very different from the goals of the speaker. If you are speaking and assume your listeners are motivated to understand, you may be very wrong!

Set goals before you listen. What do you want to gain from the time you are investing?

By the way, I don't see any of these motivations as necessarily being wrong. Most of us enter listening situations for a variety of reasons. I think at some time I have gone to church for almost every reason on the previous list! As speakers, we need to realize that listeners bring their own agenda. As listeners, we need to clearly identify our listening agenda, our goals.

Requirements of Listening to Solve Problems

In this book we are most interested in communication for solving problems. Listening to get information so that we can solve problems in our lives is complicated.[1] It requires us to:

- focus our attention,

- understand the message,

- store information in memory (or write it down),

- retrieve it from memory (or find and correctly interpret the notes),

- evaluate the information, and

- perform the act. (This also involves things like time, money, ability, freedom, and authority.)

Ethical Point
To habitually hear good information without taking action is deceiving. We may feel righteous because we attend church or read the Bible, but hearing without acting results in deception (see James 1:23) and spiritual insensitivity (see Romans 1:18-32).

Let's take the "boyfriend, girl-friend" example found earlier in this chapter. They gave each other their attention for their brief conversation. They remembered it. They decided to act on it, and were able to do so. There was only one small problem: each had a different meaning about which side was the "front" of the library.

On the other hand, "Frank and Mary" were so busy talking that they never focused on what the other was saying. I have often experienced a similar effect when sitting in a boring lecture. It's hard to maintain attention.

Focus Attention

Here are some practical pointers about how to focus your attention more effectively.

- Be clear about your goals. If your goal is to relax or be entertained — enjoy. But don't approach a lecture as you would a sitcom. Since the average person spends almost eight hours a day being entertained through the mass media, we are habituated to a passive, "entertain me," mode. Gathering information requires a different mind-set. Expect to work. Focusing your attention requires effort.

- What's in it for me? If you are going to invest an hour of your time to listen to a speech, clarify to yourself at the beginning *why* you are doing this. Are you looking for some specific information? What is it? What kind of use could you make of it? Glance over an outline if one is available. Try to develop some curiosity about the points being made. Throughout the talk ask yourself how you can use the information. Write down information you can use.

Regularly expose yourself to new ideas, new art forms, etc., so you become more interested in all of God's creation.

- Develop an inquisitive mind-set. Cultivate a sense of wonder about every aspect of God's creation. Eagerly expose yourself to new ideas, novel art forms, fresh ways of viewing truth, different disciplines. To a mind that is really alive, very little is dull, but to a small mind almost everything is boring. Someone once said there is no such thing as an uninteresting topic; there are only uninteresting people.

- The physical setting may help. I have found when counseling students it's better for me to leave my desk and move to another part of my office where I have a small table and chairs. That way I escape all the distracting materials on my desk and can concentrate more of my energy on listening. I'm usually in the middle of something else when students come by, so I have to make a deliberate effort to "change gears" and listen actively. Making the move physically helps me change gears mentally.

Sit close to the speaker where there will be fewer distractions.

For the same reason my wife and I choose to sit near the front in church. The pastor seems more animated when we're closer to him, and knowing he can see us if we are not paying attention gives us a little added motivation!

■ Don't be thinking of your next response while the other person is talking. In my television production class the students were doing interviews. One young man was interviewing a star of the women's tennis team. He didn't know her very well and hadn't prepared enough questions. He was frantically trying to think of another question after he asked her why she had decided to get into tennis. So he missed her mood change as she said, with heartbreak in her voice, that her brother had been killed in an accident. She had chosen to excel in tennis as a tribute to him. She stopped suddenly, choking with emotion.

Not having heard any of this, he came back brightly, "That's terrific. And how do you expect to do in this weekend's tournament?" The tone of his response seemed so inappropriate that a noticeable gasp escaped from the other class members, and of course he was aghast when he heard the playback.

Listen to the other person carefully. Don't be thinking of your next response.

■ Paraphrase back to the other person what has just been said. You could start with something like:

"So you feel that. . . ."
"Did I understand you to say that. . . ."
"Let's see if I understand what you're saying. . . ."
In addition to helping you concentrate your attention, this is also a good test for understanding. Use it frequently.

Paraphrase what the other person says. This helps you pay attention and check your understanding.

When you are part of a listening group, or you are reading, try to write down the main points in *other words* than those used by the writer/speaker. This is much more involving than just writing down some of the speaker's own words.

■ Figure out where the speaker is coming from. Try to figure out the speaker's background. What prejudices might result from this background? What significant perspectives is the speaker missing? What is he/she *not* saying, intentionally or unintentionally?

Know the speaker's background and intentions.

Be careful not to go too far in this direction though. Don't get so wrapped up in studying the communicator that you miss the communication. Also, be careful not to reject truth out-of-hand just because you are put off by some aspects of the communicator. Even if you know a speaker to be wrong in some particulars, he/she may be right on others.

■ Figure out where the speaker is going. Discover the speaker's main points. Paraphrase them. Try not to get buried in an avalanche of supporting detail and miss the big points.

Write down important points you can use. Don't try to write down everything.

- Take notes, but don't overdo it.

    Don't:
    (1) try to write down everything, or
    (2) write down the exact words the speaker uses.

    Do:
    (1) paraphrase the main points, and
    (2) write down source references you may need to do further study.

    You've probably heard it said that, "a lecture is a means by which the professor's notes are transcribed into the notebooks of the students without going though the mind of either." Slavish, detailed note-taking can interfere with understanding the point of the talk.

- Don't fake attention. Pretending to pay attention is a skill most of us have learned entirely too well. We look in the direction of the speaker, sit still, fix a placid smile on our faces — and our minds are miles away. This posture hurts us because we do not benefit from the talk, and it adds to the speaker's frustration because we don't respond appropriately. It's a lie and a bad habit many of us need to overcome.

■ ■ ■ ■ ■ ■ ■

A husband reads a paper as his wife chatters. He grunts periodically. She feels devalued. He might better say, "Honey, I need a few minutes to relax with the paper. Could we talk in a half-hour or so? I want to be able to give you my full attention."

■ ■ ■ ■ ■ ■

A college student reads a book as he talks to his parents on the phone. He is trying to fake interest. How much better for him to say, "I'm sorry, I've got to prepare for a test right now. Could I call you back tonight?"

■　■　■　■　■　■

If you're too tired or just not interested in a talk it's more honest and beneficial to stay home than to go and fake attention.

> **Ethical Point**
> Faking attention is a kind of flattery which is false positive feedback. Flattery is condemned in Scripture. (See Proverbs 29:5.)

■ Actively give feedback. Feedback is information you give back to speakers, either while they are speaking or afterward. Giving feedback makes the communication situation more interesting, honest, and valid for all concerned.

Verbal Feedback

In one-to-one or small group situations, ask questions, tell the communicator you agree or disagree or don't understand. Decide you are going to be an active participant in the process. Don't be afraid to interrupt, especially to seek clarification.

Break the habit of pretending to pay attention. Instead, let the speaker know your reactions, either in words or gestures.

In a public speaking, written, or mediated (radio, TV) situation, write or phone your feedback in. The habit of responding to mediated messages will make you a much better listener, and will tend to correct errors the speakers may be making.

Nonverbal Feedback

In face-to-face situations plan to sit erect, perhaps leaning forward, look the speaker squarely in the eye, nod periodically to show you understand or agree, laugh at jokes, and look puzzled when you don't understand. If you are actively giving feedback, and especially if you are anywhere near the front of the room, most speakers will find you. From time to time they will look directly at you because you are giving them feedback they need to know how they are doing. You will be much more involved with the talk, and find it much more interesting. In fact, it will probably be more interesting because you will encourage the speaker with your interest.

- Train yourself to concentrate. Be aware of your mind's tendency to wander and quickly bring it back. You might practice by selecting a verse, setting a timer for three minutes, and disciplining yourself to think of nothing else but that verse. Do this daily for 10 days and your power of concentration will improve markedly.

Increase your power of concentration by practicing.

Understand the Message

Assuming you practice the above principles to increase your attention, your ability to listen and thus understand material should dramatically improve. Now let's focus on some additional tools to help you better listen and understand what the speaker intended.

What's meant by *understanding?*

Let's think about what happens when I try to translate a thought from my mind to yours. As I write this, I'm sitting at the keyboard of my computer pressing keys which cause symbols to appear on my monitor. Similar symbols now appear in the book before you. The symbols are letters of a type the Romans concocted. The particular arrangement of the letters we recognize as words of the English language, a system of symbols understood by many millions of people around the world.

Because you know English, you will have no trouble understanding what I mean if I write the word, *dog*. You will understand that I am referring to a four-legged animal, a common household pet. So far so good.

The problem comes because you cannot fully understand what I mean by that word. You didn't know about my boyhood pet, "Nippy," who was poisoned by burglars on our Oregon ranch. You didn't experience the tears as we buried him in the side yard and engraved a crude headstone over the site.

You also wouldn't know about the feisty old cocker spaniel who bit my small son in the face and nearly took out his eye. Then there was Duchess, a cuddly little puppy I brought home for the kids, who grew up into probably the ugliest of all dog-kind. Still another family dog was run over by a truck. Tears still come to my eyes when I think of my 10-year-old son sitting on the curb while his pet dog died in his arms.

Dog means all of that to me, and more. While I can convey a general impression of what I mean by words, there is no way I can convey to you fully what any symbol means to me. You would need to have had exactly the same experiences I had. You cannot fully understand me, nor I you.

Words don't actually carry meaning. They only elicit some approximation of similar meaning in another person. David Berlo[2] put it succinctly: "Meanings are in people." That is, the relationship between the symbol (the word *dog* for example) and the thing it refers to (an actual dog) is in the mind of each person. Because my experience with dogs is different from yours, I will create a somewhat different picture in my mind and probably very different feelings.

This flies in the face of what we were taught in grade school. My teachers insisted I use words in the "correct" way. This is beneficial, of course, because it helps to standardize usage. If we all use words in standard ways, we have a better chance of understanding each other. But who defines what is correct? The best word for any given individual is one that brings to his mind a good approximation of the meaning you have in your mind. Unfortunately, that might be different words for different people.

The problem is, we believe if we use the "correct" words, everyone should understand us and feel the same things we do. We get short-tempered with people when they don't "get it." If we "see" something clearly, why can't they? Sometimes we feel they are just being difficult, insensitive, or obstinate. A wife gets angry with a husband because he just doesn't "understand" something that is perfectly obvious to her. He hasn't a clue, but she feels it's so obvious he is just being stubborn.

Remember the story of the girlfriend and boyfriend earlier in this chapter? Which one was wrong? This building, because of the way it has been added onto several times, has four sides, all of which look like fronts! Fixing blame doesn't help in a time like this. It just makes one person feel a little better and the other a lot worse. It's better to figure out where the communication broke down, learn something, have a good laugh, and go on.

"Meanings are in people" implies there are no perfect words. No matter how carefully you choose them, words will never convey exactly what you have in mind. They will sometimes bring up a very different meaning. You shouldn't be surprised, then, when you fail to communicate. Knowing this, you won't blame the other person for failing to understand.

Tell the other person what you understand and ask if that is what was intended.

If we realize how tenuous understanding is, we will be more likely to give and seek feedback, to check our perceptions. We will expect others to misunderstand us and will make allowances for it.

Here are some specific things you can do to improve understanding.

- Don't jump to conclusions. Realize your first perception of what the person is trying to convey is not totally right, and could even be totally wrong. Instead, hold the idea tentatively, as a theory to be tested and confirmed by further information.

- Look at the context. The person's background, his/her general topic, and other clues may help you close in on the meaning.

- Seek feedback. If appropriate, test your understanding by saying something like:

"If I understand you correctly, you want me to. . . ."
"So, I take it you are saying. . . ."
"Let me see if I am understanding you correctly. You said. . . ."
The source of the communication (the sender) should do the same.
"I'm not sure if I made myself clear. Would you tell me what you understand?"
"I think I may have confused you. Would you tell me what you think I was trying to say?"
The temptation is to simply ask, "Understand?" or something similar. However, this is often not effective because (1) the receiver may not know he does not understand and (2) the receiver doesn't wish to appear stupid or inattentive. It is much more effective to ask *what* the receiver understood than *if* he understood.

Seek feedback by asking the receiver what she understood.

Even when something seems unclear, I am sometimes reluctant to give feedback or ask for clarification because I don't want to seem dumb. Too often the communicator asks, "OK?" and I think I can figure it out later, so I nod yes. That, of course, is a lie, told because of pride. How much better to honestly say, "I'm not sure I understand," and ask for clarification.

Ethical Point
Pretending you understand when you don't is deceptive. Swallow your pride and be truthful when you don't understand.

But the worst form of misunderstanding happens when I feel sure I understand correctly! It's a good idea to seek feedback even when you feel confident you understand! Form the habit of routinely checking your perception by paraphrasing your understanding back to the speaker. This will result in a great increase in communication effectiveness. It is most important to clarify such matters as things you are going to do and meeting times and places. This helps you to be a person of your word, whose "yes is yes."

Admit it when you don't understand. If you're not sure, tell the person what you understand, and ask if that is what was intended.

- Delay judgment. We humans have a bad habit of jumping to conclusions. Proverbs 18:17 bears this out, "The first to present his case seems right, till another comes forward and questions him." When we shift from trying to understand to judging the validity of what's said, it's likely we will misunderstand the message.

Of course we need to judge whether what we hear is the truth. Scripture is full of admonitions to do so. I'm greatly concerned that many Christians just absorb television shows, movies, and popular magazines without careful reflection on the truthfulness of the messages they convey.

What I'm trying to point out here is that there are two distinct functions, understanding and judging. Both are necessary. But if judgment starts too soon, it may interfere with understanding.

If you've done any teaching or public speaking, it's happened to you. A guy comes up to you afterward and takes strong exception to a point you made. He has Scripture verses to back him up. The problem is, he totally misunderstood what you were saying because he stopped listening and started judging.

Here's a helpful technique for one-to-one communication, especially within marriage. Frank and Mary, mentioned earlier, could profit from it. Frank first *listens without interruption*. When Mary is done, he paraphrases back to her his understanding of her words. She corrects his paraphrase until she is satisfied he correctly understands her.

> **Ethical Point**
> Christians are cautioned to judge carefully and justly. (See Matthew 7:1-2; John 7:24; Romans 2:1; Romans 14:13; 1 Corinthians 6:2; and James 4:11.)

Only then is he allowed to say whether he agrees or disagrees. At this point she must listen to him without interruption, then paraphrase back to him her understanding. This process separates the understanding and judging functions. Many problems disappear when we really listen to each other and work first at understanding before we begin judging.

Try to understand fully *before* you decide if you agree or disagree.

■ Understanding the feelings. In much communication the words by themselves don't give us the whole picture. How the words are said tells us more. Nonverbal aspects such as tone of voice, loudness, speed, pitch, and inflection patterns tell us how to interpret the words. It's not unusual, for example, for us to say something we mean to be interpreted as the exact opposite of what the words say. For example, someone might say a woman was a "great cook" but say it in such a way with inflection and rolling of the eyes that we understand the speaker to mean she is far from being a great cook.

In written communication, such as this book, I must try to capture everything in words, since that's all I have. In conversation, I have much more: facial expressions, gestures, voice qualities, clothing, even the setting. These contribute to understanding.

The problem with nonverbal aspects of communication is that they are even harder to interpret than words. We can use nonverbal communication when we want to be able to deny our intent. I have noticed that many of my single friends find it difficult to ask for a date. Instead they show their interest by "flirting" nonverbally. If the other person doesn't take the bait, they can pretend they were just being friendly.

Watch for nonverbal behavior that seems to contradict the spoken words. It may indicate that the speaker is not being honest.

While words can express emotion and nonverbal behavior can convey thoughts (such as nodding yes), it is more common the other way around. One interesting aspect of nonverbal behavior is that it's harder to control. We can choose our words very carefully, but it's harder to control our tone of voice, facial expressions, posture, breathing, etc. It's especially useful to look for nonverbal behavior that seems *inconsistent* with the words spoken. This suggests the speaker is not being honest.

Much has been written on how to interpret nonverbal behavior. Much of it is not very reliable. If you see behavior that seems inconsistent with a person's words, you might invite the person to verbalize the feelings. You can say something like:

"How do you feel about that?"

"You seem to be nervous (angry, etc.). Can you tell me about it?"

"You seem really happy today!"

Some people are not very aware of their feelings, or may discount or deny them. If a friend is very nervous or near tears, for example, I wouldn't accept at face value her insistence that nothing is wrong. But of course it's her choice whether she wishes to talk about it.

Develop empathy by thinking about the situation another person is in, then imagine how you would feel in the same situation.

The skill of *empathy* is helpful. Empathy is the ability to emotionally put yourself in another person's situation. Paul referred to this skill in 1 Corinthians 9:22 when he talked about becoming all things to all people. You develop empathy by considering another person's plight, then imagining how you would feel if you were in the same situation. With practice you can get to the point where you experience some of the pain the other person is going through. You are not pretending to feel the pain. You actually do.

A way of developing empathy is to find a similar situation in your own life, and then recall how you felt. But don't talk about your past hurt too much, or you will seem to be saying, "Snap out of it, we all go through tough stuff."

A danger in empathy is that your past situation, or the situation as you imagine it, is different from the current situation of your friend. Don't get so wrapped up in your own past or present hurts that you fail to understand the current situation of your friend.

We also need to "Rejoice with those who rejoice" (Rom. 12:15). I think that's even harder because envy raises its ugly head. I remember when a man who worked under me was promoted to be my boss. I had trouble rejoicing with him because I thought I should have gotten the promotion! Eventually I realized that the decision was the right one to make the best use of both our gifts, but for a while I was hurt. Helping others celebrate requires faith in the goodness and justice of God.

**Pay attention to feelings as much as words.
If appropriate, ask questions that will help
the speaker express his or her feelings in words.**

Store and Retrieve Information

Most of the time we are not in a situation where we can act on information the moment we hear it. We must somehow remember or otherwise store the information for future reference if it is to be of any value.

In the sermons I have heard and workshops I have attended, I have heard some really good ideas that I intended at the time to incorporate into my life. The vast majority of these I have simply forgotten or ignored. That puts me in the category of being a "hearer" but often not a "doer" of the Word. James

1:22 says, "Do not merely listen to the Word, and so deceive yourselves. Do what it says."

That gets to me. I hear much truth, but don't do it very well. If I paid attention to a message and understood it, I must find a way to remember it so I can put it into practice.

This is not simple. There are too many good ideas. I go to church, listen to Christian radio, read Christian books and magazines, attend the chapel at the college where I teach, and attend several conferences and workshops every year. How can I remember and act on so many ideas?

> **Ethical Point**
> Hearing and knowing truth without taking appropriate action is wrong.

Obviously I can't do them all. I must separate the wheat from the chaff. It's often a choice between the good and the best. We'll discuss evaluation a bit later, but some degree of evaluation can happen even as I hear the ideas. Some sermons don't apply to me. I'm already a Christian and my children are grown, so sermons aimed at conversion or parenting don't particularly apply to me.

Some ideas seem good at the time I hear them, but upon later reflection I'm less inclined to act on them. But there are a few really good ideas that I fully intend to follow through on. I must somehow get enough of the details to stick in my mind, recall them at some convenient time, and then do them.

Communication research literature shows a large disparity between people's intentions and their actions.[3] There are many reasons for this, but memory is an important factor.

Write down good ideas.
You probably won't remember them otherwise.

Here are some strategies to help you remember.

■ Associate the new idea with something familiar. Try to think how this new information is similar or related to something you already know. Think how it is similar or different.

■ Visualize the idea. Try to form a vivid picture in your mind of the idea. Jesus often used this technique. Consider the Parable of the Sower.⁴ Instead of abstractly talking about the different degrees of receptivity among people, He gave us visual pictures that help us remember His point.

■ Apply the idea. Think of a practical problem you have or might have and how you can use this idea to solve it. Be as concrete as you can.

■ Act on the idea. When you can, do something to use the idea. When you hear the idea, think of an application, then do it.

■ Understand the idea. It's hard to remember and act on something you don't understand. Figure it out or ask for clarification. If it doesn't make sense now, there is little chance you will remember enough to be able to figure it out later.

■ Explain the idea to someone else.

■ Remind yourself. Phone your answering machine at home or work, change a ring to an unfamiliar finger, stick a note in your wallet, in your car, on your computer screen, or a place where you can't miss it.

■ Use a memory device. Form an acrostic of first letters of key words. If you must remember a list in order, use this old device:

1 – Bun	6 – Sticks
2 – Shoe	7 – Heaven
3 – Tree	8 – Gate
4 – Door	9 – Line
5 – Hive	10 – Hen

Make an idea easier to remember by thinking about it, fully understanding it, visualizing it, applying it to a problem you have, and explaining it to someone else.

These are easy to remember because they rhyme. The trick is to form a vivid mental picture that includes the item from the list above and the item you are to remember. If your grocery list is hamburger, grape soda, lettuce, and ice cream, for example, you could remember it this way: A bun (from the list) with a large, still-wrapped package of hamburger in it (make it vivid), a shoe full of awful-looking grape soda, a tree laden down with heads of lettuce, and a door made up of a giant slab of melting ice cream.

- Concentrate on one item at a time. When you hear a good idea, work hard to understand and remember it. The speaker may go on, but it's better to remember one good idea than to forget two!

Expand your powers of memory by learning techniques of reminding yourself and by using memory devices.

Evaluate Information

It's not possible to remember every good idea you hear. Fortunately, it's not necessary. Besides the note-taking strategies

37

mentioned earlier, some of the following techniques will relieve your mind.

- Write down key ideas only. There is no point in writing down things you probably can't use, and too much note-taking will interfere with your understanding.

- Transcribe your notes soon. Rewrite rough notes taken during a lecture or interview into a more meaningful form before you forget what they mean. This also gives you a chance to review and evaluate the ideas, and to plan to execute the worthwhile ones.

- Send a note of confirmation. Suppose you have met with another person and one or both of you agreed to do certain things. Soon after the meeting, write down your understanding of who is to do what by when, and send it to the other person. Say that this is your best recollection of the agreement and ask for correction or clarification if needed.

- Calendar the idea. If I have a meeting, I usually put it in the calendar book I carry. It's also a good idea to put other worthwhile things you want to do on the calendar even if they don't have to be done at any particular time.

Rewrite your original notes as soon as possible. Calendar a time to act on the idea.

Perform an Action

For some listening, the benefit is received during the communication itself, and no further action is required. If your goal is worship or entertainment, the benefit is derived during the communication itself.[5]

Much communication, however, is valueless if nothing is done because of it. That does not mean the communication has failed if action does not follow immediately. It may also be that a given communication does not bring action by itself, but when combined with other factors eventually results in action. The Bible shows a process of planting, watering, and growth which takes place over time.[6] Any given action may be the result of many messages, so it's quite difficult to say which messages are effective and which are not.

However, you can increase your personal effectiveness by deliberately choosing to act or not to act. Here are some factors to consider when making the choice.[7]

- Is the action compatible with my understanding of Scripture?

- Relative advantage. Compared to other choices available to you, what advantages does this choice offer? Sometimes this is called the "cost/benefit ratio."

- Can I try it? You can try some things, such as a change of toothpaste, with little cost or risk. Others, such as marriage, by their very nature require long-term commitment up front.

- Does it fit in? Will I have to make other changes in my life to adapt to this change? Am I willing to do so?[8]

Before taking action, evaluate the idea in terms of its compatibility with Scripture, its advantages, whether you can try it with minimal cost or commitment, and how many other changes you would have to make to adopt this idea.

Chapter Summary

As James says, if we are hearers only and not doers, we deceive ourselves. We also waste time and harden ourselves to truth. Purposeful listening is hard work. We must give our attention, concentrate on the message, and not assume we have correctly understood it without testing through feedback. We must then work to remember it and/or write it down. We must evaluate the benefits and costs, and if we still find it beneficial, do it.

Receiving communication is more important than sending it because we do so much more of it. Knowing how to be a good "listener" also gives us information about being an effective sender.

1. Adapted from William McGuire, "The Nature of Attitudes and Attitude Change," in vol. 3 of *The Handbook of Social Psychology,* 2nd ed., G. Lindzey and E. Aronson, eds. (Reading, Mass.: Addison-Wesley, 1969), 136–314.

2. David K. Berlo, *The Process of Communication* (New York: Holt, Rinehart, and Winston, 1960), 175.

3. M. DeFleur and F.R. Westie, "Attitudes as a Scientific Concept," *Social Forces:* 42 (1963): 17–31.

4. See Matthew 13:1-23.

5. Because of this similarity, there may be some confusion between worship and entertainment. A distinction could be made that worship is to give pleasure to God while entertainment is for the purpose of receiving pleasure for one's self.

6. See 1 Corinthians 3:6.

7. Adapted from Everett Rogers and F. Floyd Shoemaker, *Communication of Innovations,* 2nd ed. (New York: Free Press, 1960), 135–57.

8. When we ask people to "only believe," we should perhaps warn them that true belief in Jesus as Savior and Lord will change virtually every aspect of their lives!

CHAPTER TWO

Know Your Audience

You can improve your communication most dramatically by learning about your audience.

If you know your audience, you can tailor your message to meet particular needs. You will learn that some times are better than others for giving your message, and that some people are more likely to respond than others.

Jesus understood that people respond differently. In the Parable of the Sower,[1] Jesus taught that even a perfect seed, God's Word, will not always bear fruit. Some seed fell in fertile soil, some landed on rocky soil, some fell among thorns, and some was snatched away by birds.

To put it another way, qualities in the receiver and in the reception situation make a difference in how well the message is received and acted upon. If people ignore God's perfect message, they will certainly ignore our less-than-perfect messages!

The parable also teaches another, more difficult lesson. After He had spoken the parable, His disciples came to Jesus and asked, "Why do you speak to the people in parables?" He answered, "The knowledge of the secrets of the kingdom of heaven has been given to you, but not to them." Jesus was choosing to give more truth to those who were receptive, but to withhold it from those who were not.

Jesus was doing what salespeople call "qualifying" a prospect. So as not to waste time on those who are not likely to buy, skilled salespeople ask a prospect some questions before they start the sales talk. Based on the prospect's answers, the salespeople decide whether to make a "pitch." Part of being an effective communicator is finding which people are more likely to respond, and at what times they will respond.

Spend most of your time communicating with people who are likely to respond.

Why Do People Listen?

People are more likely to listen if they think what you are saying will be *useful* to them.

Jesus sometimes met a physical need to gain the opportunity to address the deeper spiritual need. For example, when He spoke to a Samaritan woman by a well,[2] she was amazed because His action violated a cultural taboo. Then He spoke to her of "living water" which she saw as something to permanently meet her physical thirst. Because she was seeking a solution to a *felt* need, she gave Jesus her attention, and He had the opportunity to address her deeper needs.

Two principles emerge from Jesus' actions:

- People are not equally ready to hear. Direct your messages to those who are more ready.

- People will be willing to listen to the extent they believe that what you are offering meets a need. The more intensely they feel a need, the more likely they are to listen.

Meet people's felt needs to gain the opportunity to address their spiritual needs.

While doing research at a secular university, I gave a group of students a test. They were to sort a group of value statements into order of importance for them personally. In the list there were items such as making a good income, having a comfortable life, and being respected. Among the statements was one that had to do with finding salvation or eternal life. To my surprise, all but one of these students listed this one dead last!

If I were to try to attract an audience of these young collegians to a talk on "How to Have Eternal Life," most would find something they would rather do. A talk on "How to Enjoy Life," or "How to Earn a Lot of Money without Working Very Hard," might draw well!

By the way, the one exception, the student who did not list "finding eternal life" last, listed it first. She was a beautiful young woman who had recently been diagnosed with terminal cancer. Knowing she was near the end of this life made finding eternal life a high priority. Timing is important.

Winning an Audience

Usually people are not forced to listen to us. They choose to do so for a variety of reasons. By understanding these reasons we can better attract and hold an audience.

Using Incidental Listening

When people hear a message without really intending to, we call it "incidental listening." You don't watch television to see the commercials, but you still see them. If you have a message the audience does not want to hear, you can present it as incidental to information or entertainment they want. You can:

- invite people to a party and have someone give a brief testimony at the end,

- put Christian spots on the popular music stations in your area, and

- share your faith where others can overhear you. While doing research for a film, I met Charles "Tex" Watson, the former mass murderer and member of the "Manson family." Charles has a remarkable testimony of how he came to the Lord partly because of a conversation he overheard in the visiting room in prison.

Ethical Point
Don't attract an audience by promising benefits unless you fulfill your promise.

Is this ethical? Is it honest to "slip in" something people don't particularly want to hear as part of something they do want to hear?

Since Jesus used this technique, we know we must be on solid ground. But let's notice some details.

- The benefit promised must be real. We would be wrong to attract a listener by promising a benefit and then not providing it.

- We must not deceive.

- We must not coerce. People must be free to opt out at any time.

Position your message
where people will encounter it
even if they are not seeking it.

Using a "Power" Situation

This technique for winning an audience is particularly sensitive because of possible ethical problems. If you control something another person needs, you have power over that person. For example, if you are an employer, you control the person's pay. If you are a teacher, you control the student's grade. In a power relationship you must carefully separate those areas over which you have legitimate control from those in which you do not. An employer has the right to expect an employee to do his work correctly, but does not have the right to dictate how the employee spends his free time.

To put this issue into perspective, think of it this way. Everyone belongs to God in the sense that He made us and controls the universe. Yet when Jesus came to earth, He respected the right of His own creation to choose to reject Him. He presented the truth plainly. Then, though He had all power, He allowed people to make their own choices.[3]

> **Ethical Point**
> Don't use a power relationship to influence people in an area unrelated to the legitimate power relationship.

When you have a power relationship over a person, you must be careful about even making suggestions because these may be interpreted as demands. For example, it would be wrong for a male employer to ask a female employee to go out to dinner with him, unless there is a legitimate business reason to do so. The woman might assume her job or promotion is at stake if she declines. This could be considered sexual harassment.

Be careful not to use your power illegitimately to force your views on other people.

Therefore, when you give spiritual counsel to non-Christian employees or students, do it carefully. Make sure they understand you are not using your position to force them to take actions they would not choose on their own.

DO:
- put up a poster of a Christian activity on a bulletin board that is available to any employee for posting events;

- converse naturally about your personal beliefs when it is clear you are not suggesting or requiring a particular response;

- answer questions from employees;

- live a pure, clean, dynamic Christian life that will make others want to ask how you do it!

DON'T:
- ask an employee to an evangelistic service, unless the employee has previously expressed interest and will not see it as coercion;

- suggest an employee read the Bible, watch a program, etc.;

- present the plan of salvation (unless requested by employee).

Using "Attractiveness"

In this situation people in the audience choose to listen because of their attraction to you rather than because of your content. What kind of person will be attracted to you? Generally these will be people who believe you value the same things they do.

People who see you as attractive will desire to have a relationship with you. They will want to listen to you. If you promote an idea they don't agree with, they may change their mind, either about the issue or about you. They may decide they don't like you as much as they once did.

Is there any ethical problem with using your attractiveness to get people to listen to you? An ethical problem arises only if you promise or imply some benefit or relationship you do not provide, or you are not the person you appear to be.

Let your audience know when you value the same things they do.

Satisfying Felt Needs

Usually the best reason people have for listening is that the message meets a felt need. By "needs" I don't necessarily mean deep, true needs, but rather what the person feels at the moment to be a need. We are talking about needs as *perceived* by an intended audience member.

My perceptions and God's knowledge of what is really true often disagree. I may *feel* strongly that I "need" a fancy new car. Even if this is not a real need as known by God, I will still be motivated to pay attention to information about new cars.

Categories of Needs

Physical	Emotional	Social	Intellectual	Aesthetic	Spiritual
Food Water Air Shelter Clothing Exercise Medical care	To feel loved To be able to feel and express emotions such as love, anger, hate, and fear To not be too controlled by emotions	To be accept- ed To have friends To belong To be respected	To think To solve problems To figure things out To make sound decisions	To enjoy beauty such as art or nature To create beauty by such activities as singing, writing, painting, performing, or other artistic endeavors	To have a sense of purpose for this life and beyond To know there is something of signi- ficance beyond this life To know God

Our ideas of what we need depend on many factors. These include such things as deprivation (we feel hungry if we haven't eaten for a long time), time of day, time of life, societal influences, and advertising.

The needs can be long-term, such as advice about retirement or eternal life. Or they can be short-term, such as the desire to have a snack, or for a change of mood. The needs can be in any realm: physical, emotional, intellectual, aesthetic, social, or spiritual.

A Hierarchy of Needs

If we are to meet felt needs, we must first identify them. We all have dozens, maybe hundreds of needs of which we are more or less aware. Some are very much in our thinking; some are in the background. More needs are common to all of us, however, the urgency or salience of a particular need may change with such factors as age, occupation, where we live, and how much money we have.

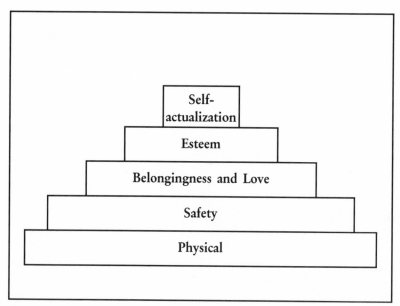

Figure 3.1

Psychologist Abraham Maslow[4] helps us understand why we don't all feel needs in the same way. Notice in figure 3.1 that physical needs are at the bottom, making them foundational. If we don't have food, water, or air to breathe, all other needs become unimportant. On the other hand, when our physical needs are reasonably well met, we don't think about them very much. Our attention shifts to the next higher need, "safety." People who live in rough neighborhoods or who are experiencing storms, floods, or earthquakes have a strong need for safety.

Many people are found at the next level, "Belongingness and Love." Their physical needs are met well enough, and they feel safe, but they don't feel as if they belong, or are loved. According to Maslow they will be strongly motivated to find love.

Most popular music, television shows, and movies deal with this need. Teenagers feel these needs intensely because they are going through a phase in life in which they are detaching themselves from their parents' control. As they break away, they devalue their parents' love and must find other ways to feel they belong and are loved.

For some the search for love and acceptance is lifelong, never satisfied. Some are so perfectionistic they could never be satisfied by the love of any real person. Others are too fearful to enter into loving relationships.

Most of us experience times that bring us back to feeling an intense need to be loved and accepted. Divorce or the unfaithfulness of a spouse, a broken engagement, or even a failed friendship may make us feel unloved. Even a sharp word from a spouse or friend can cause us to wonder if we are loved. Finding that some friends got together without inviting us makes us feel we don't "belong."

Those who do feel loved, according to Maslow, experience a need for esteem. This level appears in some ways to be a continuation of the previous seeking for love and acceptance, but on a higher level. To be esteemed is to be valued, to be thought of as important, and to have a sense of self-acceptance.

The highest level, which Maslow says few achieve, is self-actualization. This is the satisfaction that comes from giving oneself over to creative activity or significant achievement – to create something lasting and worthwhile.

Be aware that different people have different needs at different times.

It seems to me that Solomon reflects the pressure of self-actualization in the Book of Ecclesiastes. He observes the futility of all his human effort. He rightly concludes the only really significant things are the simple satisfaction of work and relationships, and especially the relationship with God.

As Christians we understand that God is the supplier of all our needs at each level.[5] We can only achieve anything *eternally* meaningful through our relationship to Him. But most of us do not experience all that we know we have in Christ. In Romans, Paul tells of the struggle to bring our walk into alignment with our status as dead in Christ and resurrected to new life.[6]

Find a felt need and fill it.

If we who know Christ still struggle to feel loved and significant, those without Christ struggle even more. If we can figure out at what level our audience members are, we can customize our message to speak to their particular felt needs.

For example, we all know that "God is love." The words are easy to say, but we can hardly begin to understand the depth of their meaning. Let's consider Steve,[7] age 42. His wife recently announced she was leaving him for another man. In the divorce settlement he lost his home and was granted visitation of his kids alternate weekends. It's troubling for him to see them because it reminds him of his failed marriage. Also, there is not much to do at his apartment, so he takes them miniature golfing, which they all seem to just tolerate.

He is floundering at work too. He is so disoriented he can hardly concentrate. As a salesperson, his diminished self-confidence has taken its toll. His commissions this year are only about half last year's. He is going to lose a large bonus he has received in previous years. He needs the money to pay child support beyond his own living expenses. He desperately wants to be loved, but the pain and hurt of his broken marriage cause him to be suspicious of the women he meets.

Unaccustomed to being single, Steve feels awkward when getting together with old friends. Most of them knew Steve and his wife as a couple. Most of his old friends don't call him, and some don't even return his calls. He feels really alone.

Get to know the stories of the people to whom you are ministering.

How do we tell Steve that God loves him? The words, straight out, will seem like mockery. "If God loves me," he thinks, "why did He do this to me?" Though Steve wouldn't consider himself "religious," he prayed desperately that his marriage wouldn't end. Now he feels betrayed by God.

Steve feels an intense need to be loved, but he does not identify this with a need for God. By showing Steve love, we may earn the opportunity to help him discover the greatest lover of all. How can we love Steve? Invite him in for a meal, or to a party. Do something with him and the kids. Give him a book or pamphlet about successful single parenting. In other words, meet him at the level of the needs he feels.

Or consider Stephanie, a successful 55-year-old physician. She has a loving husband, also a physician, two children, and three grandchildren. Everything in her life seems to be going beautifully, yet, inexplicably, she feels empty. Her work has become routine, even draining. She has achieved all her goals, and in retrospect they seem almost inconsequential. When she thinks about retirement, the concept seems boring, trivial. Together she and her husband earn about $400,000 per year, but there is nothing she can imagine buying or doing that would be meaningful to her.

Her need is to find a larger purpose in life, something she can give herself to and find deep satisfaction. Christ can give her such a purpose.

How can we help her? At first it seems too good to be true. She has money and needs a purpose. We have a purpose, but need money. It's a marriage made in heaven!

But wait! She doesn't want to give away money. It's important to her. She gains a sense of security and satisfaction from knowing how much she has. She is looking for significance, a way to accomplish something lasting and worthwhile. Perhaps we can help her use her talents to help less fortunate people, or to advise a mission hospital. Once she sees something as significant she will probably invest both time and money in it.

We need, of course, to also find a way to introduce her to the One who makes our lives significant throughout eternity.

How to Become Acquainted with Your Intended Receivers

We sometimes assume people are more similar to us than they actually are. In a sense, all communication is "cross cultural." If you are teaching high school students, their "culture" is different from yours. If you are teaching a group of recent immigrants, the differences would be more obvious, but no more real. If you think other groups of people are the same as you, you are wrong in some important ways.

Messages and communication techniques that might work very well with people like you may fall absolutely flat with others. So you need to dig in and do some hard work to find out what the people in your audience are like.

Simple Methods

- Talk *with* them, not *to* them! Arrange situations so you can interact with your intended receivers (or people similar to them) face-to-face. Your task is not to try to influence them during these conversations but to understand them. Ask questions and listen a lot. Make it safe for them to tell you what they truly believe.

- Get acquainted with their world. Visit their homes, neighborhoods, schools, factories, laundromats, churches, synagogues, etc.

- Learn from their media. Listen to their radio stations, watch their favorite television shows, read their magazines, papers, books, and even comic books.

- Become a participant in their lives. When they get to know you better, they will feel free to open up more.

Spend time with your audience members and get to know their culture and media.

More Complicated Methods

The above methods will work well for small groups, and as a beginning point for any group. If you are working with a larger group, you will also need to supplement the above methods with more formal research. For example, if you are working with a large church congregation, you will need to do some survey research. For these reasons, informal methods of getting to know your audience can be deceptive when the audience is large. You need to include formal research, including focus groups, survey research, and experimental research.

Focus Groups

This is a small group (from about 4 to 16) which you bring together to discuss your chosen topic. A professional who is not closely aligned to the organization or issue usually leads the discussion so people feel free to speak candidly. The sessions usually last two or three hours, and the respondents are often paid, or at least given a free meal.

Advantages: You can cover the issue in depth and discover troublesome areas you might have overlooked.

Disadvantages: You have a very small sample, so it is not necessarily representative.

When to use: Focus groups are best used when you are not sure what the issues are. Suppose attendance at your church has been shrinking for the past year and no one is sure why. Conducting focus groups would probably turn up the reasons. The pastor and other prominent church officials should not lead these groups so the respondents can be very candid. You might discover several problems. Unfortunately, it might not be clear which problems are the most important. Then, you would need some additional survey research.

Use focus groups to find out what the real issues are.

When an audience is larger than you can expect to get to know personally, you need research methods to avoid a common kind of error called "overgeneralization." This is a bias that creeps in when we assume that those we don't know are pretty much like those we do. This error comes about because the people we know are not an accurate cross section of the entire group. Our friends and even acquaintances tend to be similar to us. An important aspect of research is selecting an accurate cross section to study.

"Wonderful sermon, pastor," a woman gushes, then moments later crucifies both pastor and sermon to her friends. What's happening here? She gave a socially acceptable response. The front door of the church is not the place to give honest feedback, so she said what was expected, not what she thought. The pastor (teacher, performer, etc.) should be careful not to take these social amenities seriously.

Another problem with informal observation is that it gets quite complicated when the group gets large. Experience has shown that we humans are not very good at summarizing data. We tend to be too influenced by the exceptional and therefore miss the ordinary.

I see this myself when I do research. I type the data from several hundred questionnaires into the computer. Having thoroughly read all of the questionnaires, I think I should have a good idea of what to expect when the statistics come out. I am almost always surprised. You see, my thinking is often skewed by a small percentage of people who write very strong or unusual reactions.

Survey Research

Unless the group is small enough so that a census can be done, you will need to draw a sample. You will need to have someone prepare a questionnaire. Then you will need to conduct interviews, tabulate the data with a computer, and finally write a report. All of this requires some expertise to avoid inaccurate results. It is best to hire a trained researcher to at least do the research design and data analysis.

Advantages: If correctly done, survey research yields very precise and reliable information so you can make decisions with a high degree of confidence.

Use survey research when your audience is larger than you can know personally.

Disadvantages: Can be expensive and time-consuming.

When to use: Use survey research when you need to gather information to make important decisions about a group that is larger than you can know well at the personal level. Although research is costly, it is cheaper than correcting for the errors you may make without it!

Experimental Research

Suppose you want to find out which of two or more different approaches works best. For example, your ministry wants to attract large numbers of junior high students to special meetings, and you don't know which kind of advertising message would draw best. Experiment and find out!

One way would be to do what's called a "field" experiment. You place two ads and then find out which worked better. It would probably be cheaper (but maybe less accurate) to do a "lab" experiment in which you bring in a group of junior high students. Show half of them each version of the ad and see which influenced them most.

> **Ethical Point**
> Conducting a sales or evangelistic campaign under the guise of doing research is deceptive and therefore wrong!

Advantages: A survey can only find out what already is. In an experiment you can manipulate something to find out what happens.

Disadvantages: Could be costly. Can be misleading if done incorrectly.

When to use: Use experimental research when you have a considerable investment of time and/or money involved in a methodology that hasn't been tested. Testing is almost always cheaper than failure!

Research Problems to Avoid

Unless you have training in doing research, you should hire a consultant. This is not foolproof, however, because not all "consultants" are knowledgeable. Here are some errors to avoid.

Use experimental research to find out which methods work best.

- Non-random sample. If your potential audience is so large you must sample from it instead of doing a census, it is important that the sample be drawn randomly. A random sample gives you a high degree of confidence that the sample will agree closely with the entire population. A sample drawn by any other means will not be as representative. For example, suppose you ask people to volunteer to be in such a sample. You can be fairly sure those who volunteer are different from those who do not, so your study will not be valid.

- Non-response bias. After the sample is drawn, you need to work hard to get a high percentage of those selected to respond. This is a problem with mail surveys. Let's say you mail a survey out to 10,000 people, and 500 of them respond. "Well," you say, "what's wrong with that? Five hundred is a pretty decent sample size, isn't it?"

  Yes it is, but it is only 5 percent of your total. You can't assume that the tiny minority who responded is typical of the entire group. You don't know why these people chose to respond, but they may be quite different from the majority who didn't. Therefore, the study is worthless.

  If you use mailed questionnaires, you will need to follow up with more letters, phone calls, even personal calls to get the response rate up high enough. How high? That's a judgment call, but I like to get at least 70 percent.

- Leading or confusing questions. "You wouldn't be in favor of murdering poor innocent unborn babies, would

57

you?" Although I agree with the sentiment of this question, it's a terrible one for research for two reasons. First, it suggests that one answer ("no") is more appropriate or acceptable than another. Second, it uses emotionally charged terms, such as *murdering, poor, innocent,* and *babies.* Those who choose to abort them don't see them in these terms.

What's so wrong with this question? It depends on what your purpose is. If you are trying to influence opinion, it may be effective. If you are trying to find out about the opinion another person holds as honestly and accurately as possible, this question won't work. The way this is framed, it would be hard for pro-abortion people to express their opinion.

If we really want people's honest opinions, especially on sensitive issues, we must be very careful to ask questions so any response appears equally acceptable. Instead of the question above we might ask, "Regarding abortion, do you see yourself as more pro-choice or pro-life?" This uses terms acceptable to either side without forcing anyone to an extreme position.

You should also word questions clearly. Use short, familiar words and short sentences without complicated grammar.

Do research correctly if you do it at all. Poorly done research leads to false conclusions.

How Far Should I Go to Communicate?

Getting to know your audience seems like a lot of work, doesn't it? Is it worth it? How much effort do I need to spend to communicate effectively?

When God was faced with people who seemed particularly reluctant to listen, He had His servants, the prophets, do some really remarkable things to get their attention. God instructed

Hosea,[8] for example, to marry a prostitute. Then when she left him, he had to track her down and buy her back out of bondage. All this was done as an illustration of God's love. Ezekiel had to lie on his left side and cook his food over manure for 390 days to symbolize the 390 years of sin of Israel.[9]

The greatest example of all was Jesus. He left indescribable glory to come to earth and live among humanity. He put up with abuse and insults. At the end He was executed on false charges. He accepted all this injustice so He could communicate God's love.[10]

Know your audience even though it is difficult and expensive. It is the most important part of effective communication.

Chapter Summary

People don't all respond the same. Certain people at certain times are more likely to respond. Spend more of your effort with people more likely to respond.

People listen to satisfy their own needs. Find a need and meet it to earn the right to be heard. To reach people who are not motivated to hear, put your message where they will come across it incidentally.

When you are in authority over another person, it is not ethical to use that position to force on them your opinion about things not related to the job.

Others will be more attracted to you and more influenced by you if you emphasize the ways you are similar to them.

If your message meets a felt need, it is more likely to be heard. Different people have different needs at different times. We need to know the "stories" of our audience. Spend time with those you

59

are trying to reach and get to know their culture.

For groups that are larger than you can know personally, use more formal research strategies, such as focus groups, survey, or experimental research. Remember that research must be done carefully, however, or the results will be misleading.

1. Also called the Parable of the Soils. See Matthew 13:1-23.
2. See John 4:1-41.
3. See, for example, Luke 18:15-25.
4. A.H. Maslow, *Motivation and Human Behavior,* rev. ed. (New York: Harper and Row, 1970).
5. See Philippians 4:19. Note also that Paul went through a learning process (v. 11) prior to being able to make this confident statement.
6. See especially Romans 6:11.
7. A fictitious name representing a composite of several actual people.
8. See Hosea, chapters 1–3.
9. See Ezekiel 4:4-17.
10. See Philippians 2:5-8.

CHAPTER THREE

Use Feedback

W hat is feedback? Feedback is information that the receiver sends back to the sender of the message. It can take many forms.

- A quizzical look on Sally's face tells Scott that she did not understand his comment.

- A raised hand in a classroom alerts the teacher to a question.

- Letters to the editor give a reaction to the paper's editorial.

- A test lets the teacher know how much the students learned from her lessons.

Kinds of Feedback

Feedback can be positive or negative, true or false. The matrix below illustrates the outcomes of each type.

	Positive	Negative
True	True positive feedback says, "Continue on the same path. You're doing OK." And you are. It's the kind we most want. It helps us keep on the right path.	True negative feedback says, "Change course. You're going the wrong way." And you are. It's the most beneficial but perhaps the least appreciated type of feedback.
False	False positive feedback says, "You are doing OK," but you are not. We like to hear feedback like this, but it's harmful because it keeps us going in the wrong direction.	False negative feedback says, "You're going the wrong way," but you are not. We don't like to hear these words, but if we believe them we will change to the wrong course.

Both true negative or positive feedback are helpful, although we much prefer the positive. In fact, we like the feeling of positive feedback so much we tend to structure our lives so that we can receive and give positive feedback — "strokes" — even when we have to lie to do so. Sometimes the truth hurts, and we don't like either to hurt or be hurt.

The Importance of Feedback

How is the control mechanism of an elevator able to cause the car to stop precisely at the right floor? First it counts the number of turns on the winch pulling the cable to get it close. Then it switches to a sensor at each floor to do the fine adjustment. This way the system compensates for stretch in the cables and other factors that would cause the car to stop a little above or below the right place. The important thing to notice here is that there is a sensor at the point where the action is taking place, sending information back.

Only information gathered where the action is taking place is accurate enough to bring about a good result. The same is true with human systems. If we send out a lesson, sermon, or radio broadcast, for example, we need accurate feedback *from the audience,* or we may be miles away from our target.

Consider a room with a thermostat. When it gets too cool in the room, the thermostat sends an electronic message to the furnace that turns it on. In a little while it gets warm enough and the thermostat sends a message to turn the furnace off. It wouldn't do much good if the thermostat were on the furnace because then it couldn't accurately judge how warm the room was.

Now let's suppose an electrician has wired the thermostat so it gives false information. When it gets too cool, the thermostat says it's too warm, so the furnace doesn't come on, and the room just keeps getting colder. But, one warm day the thermostat says it's too cool, so the furnace switches on and keeps making the room hotter and hotter until the house finally burns down. False feedback will cause us to err on one side or the other. If followed long enough, the result will be disaster.

Think about a pilot of a small plane. Suddenly he loses his visibility. He's "socked in" with clouds. Having lost his visual feedback, he has to rely on his instruments. But, he wonders, are they accurate? Used to flying "by the seat of his pants," he doesn't fully trust his instruments, so when they say he's banking when he "feels" he is flying straight, he goes with his feelings, and flies into a mountainside. Every pilot knows you must trust your instruments and not your feelings.

Judge your effectiveness by the results in the receiver rather than by your feelings.

In a similar way we may prefer to judge the effectiveness of our communication effort based on how *we* feel afterward, which may have very little to do with our actual effectiveness. Recently, I gave my wife directions on how to get to a restaurant where she was to meet our daughter for lunch. I felt very confident that the instructions were excellent, but I had forgotten to tell her which way to go on one freeway. She, of course, went the wrong way, and I got some feedback later about the quality of my instructions!

Most of the time when we blow it we never find out. People don't speak out during a church service and say, "Pastor, I don't have a clue what you're talking about." After the service they will probably lie and say, "I enjoyed your sermon, Pastor," because they don't want to hurt the pastor's feelings.

Even during one-to-one communication people won't necessarily tell us when we have blown it. A boss tells his secretary to mail a certain memo to the board. She doesn't quite understand what he means but doesn't want to look stupid, so she tries to figure it out on her own. A week later the boss is horrified to find that a confidential internal memo was mailed to the board.

True Feedback Requires Trust

I remember a rather obnoxious young woman from college days who claimed to always tell the truth. She wasn't very popular. She often hurt people's feelings by volunteering comments such as, "That dress makes you look fat."

Because most of us care about other people's feelings, we often withhold the truth. We sometimes even tell "white lies" rather than hurt someone. A husband may not think his wife is very attractive in her new dress but will probably not tell her so. If she asks, he'll probably say, "You look fine. Come on, let's go."

Make it safe for people to tell you the truth.

We lie partly for our own protection — we don't want to have others think of us as harsh or critical. We may not be willing to admit when we don't understand something for fear of looking stupid.

Some of us don't tell the truth because we lack confidence. We don't have much trust in our perceptions or opinions. We fear that if we say what we think, we will be refuted, and then we will become embarrassed and even more lacking in confidence.

This oil of polite deception helps make the social machinery operate, but it makes finding the truth difficult. Before people will tell us the truth, they must believe we really want to hear it. They must also believe we are mature enough neither to be hurt nor to hurt them with what they tell us.

> **Ethical Point**
> A "white lie" — one designed not to hurt another person's feelings — leads to a wrong conclusion and inappropriate actions. Give the gift of honesty, even when it might hurt.

Building trust requires effort and consistency. In our personal relationships we must communicate clearly that we want to hear the truth. When someone takes the risk and gives me some true negative feedback, I should be very appreciative. If I prove myself able and willing to hear negative truth with appreciation, others will learn to trust me, and I will grow in communication ability.

If, however, I punish a truth teller by attacking or sulking, I will probably not hear negative truth from her again unless she comes to have so little regard for me that she doesn't mind hurting my feelings.

Reward people who take the risk of telling you the truth, even if the truth is unpleasant.

Corrective (true negative) feedback is perhaps the most valuable gift we can give or receive. It may also be the most costly because we risk hurting, offending, or even losing someone we care about. When someone cares enough to tell us the truth, we should tell him sincerely how much we appreciate it, even when we don't entirely agree with what he says.

Feedback-seeking Techniques

- Ask for feedback. Say things like, "Please let me know how I can improve."

- Let people be anonymous if they wish. You could pass out blank 3 x 5 cards at a Sunday School class and have people note both what they particularly like and what could be improved. Ask them not to sign the cards.

- Make feedback opportunities common. You could have cards labeled, *Feedback,* or just *Communication* in the pew racks. You could have a suggestion box.

- Ask for feedback on specific areas about which you feel uncertain.

- Ask for feedback if you are thinking about making any specific changes.

- Seek additional feedback or clarification if initial feedback is not clear. If someone comes up with a criticism that doesn't seem to make sense, discuss the idea in more detail with the individual.

- Accept responsibility for any communication breakdown. If you're misunderstood, don't let the other person feel stupid for asking for clarification. Accept responsibility by saying something like, "I'm sorry I didn't make myself clear. Thanks for giving me the chance to clear it up."

- Anticipate breakdown. Don't ask, "Do you understand?" Instead, realize what the hearer understands will often not be the same thing you intended, so say something like, "I'm not sure I made myself clear. Could you tell me what you understood me to say?" Or, "OK, let's make sure we understand each other. Where are we going to meet?"

Asking, "Do you understand?" is unwise for two reasons. First, people often think they understand when they don't. Second, even if they are not sure they understand, people don't like to appear dumb, especially to someone they like.

- Remove guilt from communication failure. If people are berated and made to feel guilty when they fail to make themselves understood, they will deny, blame others, or try to hide their botched attempts. If it's safe to fail, they will grow. A calm analysis of what went wrong is much more beneficial than assigning blame!

- In a small group situation, reward a person who seeks clarification. You could say something like, "That's a very good question," or, "I'm glad you asked that." This will encourage others to admit when they don't understand something.

- Give feedback on feedback. "So what you understood was _____, is that right?" Sometimes it takes several exchanges back and forth before both parties are convinced they understand each other.

Feedback for Large Groups

When the group size is larger than you can know personally, feedback is even more important and more difficult. In this case more formal research strategies, such as those outlined in the previous chapter, will be needed.

When Feedback Can Be Dangerous

At the beginning of this chapter, a chart shows that feedback can be positive or negative and true or false. True feedback is always helpful and false feedback is always harmful. False positive feedback is what we call flattery. It says, "Keep it up, you're doing great," when you're not. The Bible soundly condemns flattery.[1] Flattery is especially dangerous because we have a natural tendency to want to be affirmed. Satan and unscrupulous people can use this to our disadvantage.

Think of true things you can say to express support to another person. Don't lie even to spare another person's feelings.

On the other hand, the Bible gives many examples of truthful, positive feedback; that is, encouragement to keep on with a good course of action.[2] It is biblical and important to both give and receive truthful encouragement.

False negative feedback is a bit less dangerous for most of us since we naturally tend to resist criticism and change. The person most at risk to false negative feedback (saying you are on the wrong road when you are actually on the right road) is the very conscientious and tender-hearted person, or one who has very little self-confidence.

A friend of mine, who is the head of a large, Christian organization, fits this description. He is very humble and tender-hearted and is therefore frequently burdened down with the weight of undue criticism. He feels he must answer each critic, uses much time and energy in doing so, and is thus diverted from his more important tasks.

Evaluate criticism. Don't spend too much time on unfair or false criticism. Use truthful criticism to help you change in beneficial ways.

While it is admirable to be sensitive to criticism, it is also important to make an accurate judgment about its validity and not give too much attention to unjustified criticism. If we routinely ignore all criticism (as some do), we miss the most valuable feedback of all, truthful negative or corrective feedback. In other words, if we are too "thick-skinned," we miss the chance to find out where we are "blowing it" so we can change.

> **Ethical Point**
> It is wrong to give false negative or positive feedback. It is equally wrong to withhold true feedback from those to whom it is due.

The matter is made more complicated because there are two kinds of false feedback: the intentionally false and the unintentionally false. The intentionally false could be deliberate lies told to gain favor, or the "little white lies" of social convention. The unintentionally false information would come from people who are careless with facts or have themselves been misled.

Another important factor is how much the single critical view represents the opinion of most. If two or three people communicate a similar view to you in the same week, you could easily jump to the false conclusion that this is a widely held view. It's good to remember that when someone gives an opinion, she may be the only one who has the particular view, or it may be widespread; you have no way of knowing without further research. It is our human tendency to overgeneralize. When we become aware of something, we tend to think it is more prevalent than it is. Right after I bought a Toyota I saw them everywhere. I hadn't noticed them previously.

I have often heard statements such as, "For everyone who writes a letter (makes a phone call, complains, etc.) there are _____ (fill in any number you wish) who feel the same way but don't communicate it." Such statements are useless because there is no way to know what number to put in the blank unless you do some research. If you get some feedback, the only thing you know for sure is that one person feels that way. Of course even that person could be lying!

Remember, there is no way to know if criticism coming from one person is also felt by others. Don't overgeneralize.

During my days of working in radio, I witnessed the power of a few letters. If the station got even one or two letters on a certain subject, the station would often change its programming, believing the opinion was widely held. I once called a radio station to complain about a horoscope feature. They took it off!

Separating False from True Feedback

- Consider the motives. Does the person want to sell you something, or win your friendship or in some other way influence you? Take what he says with a large grain of salt!

- How well do you know the person? Trust someone you know to be trustworthy much more than strangers.

- How reasonable is the feedback? Feedback that seems well thought out and reasonable is more likely to be valid. Radical or extreme feedback is less likely to be valid.

- How representative is the feedback? Is the giver of feedback well connected socially or is she isolated? Have you received similar feedback on several occasions, or is this the first time?

- How detailed is the feedback? Does the person give dates, times, and specific instances, or is the feedback diffuse and general? Trust specific and detailed feedback more.

- Pray for wisdom.[3]

Chapter Summary

Feedback is information sent from the receiver of a message back to the source. It can be negative (that is, corrective) or positive, true or false.

In a communication situation feedback is essential. If we get accurate feedback, we can correct misunderstandings before they become serious.

It is not always easy to get accurate feedback. People do not want to risk offending us to give us truth we might not like hearing. To receive accurate feedback we need to cultivate a climate of trust. We must also actively ask for it and reward truth even when it is unpleasant.

Feedback in mass communication is even more difficult. The few people who call or write may not be representative of the entire audience. You need to regularly use research to obtain feedback from a mass audience.

1. See, for example, Proverbs 29:5; Romans 16:18; and 1 Thessalonians 2:5.
2. See, for example, Joshua 1:7; Hebrews 3:6.
3. See James 1:5.

Capture Attention

CHAPTER FOUR

Cut through
the Listeners' Fog

D o you remember the old joke about the mule? Seems a
farmer was having great trouble getting his mule to
obey him. A neighbor came over and said, "I'll bet you
five dollars I can get him to obey me with just a whisper."

"You're on," said the farmer.

The neighbor took a two-by-four and gave the mule a terrific
wallop on the side of the head.

"Hold on," said the farmer. "You said he would obey you
with just a whisper."

"He will," said the neighbor. "But first I had to get his
attention."

Human communication is pretty much the same. Your message won't affect people if they're not listening. And, as any
parent who has announced bedtime to a group of children
watching television can attest, attention tends to be highly
selective.

This book is loosely organized around a communication
model from Dr. William McGuire of the University of San
Diego.[1] Dr. McGuire's model has the following five steps:

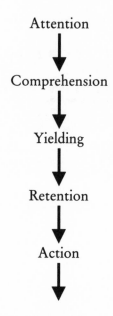

Attention

Comprehension

Yielding

Retention

Action

Capturing Listeners' Attention

Nothing happens unless you first gain the listeners' attention.

A British psychologist, Dr. Donald Broadbent[1] gives us some insight into the process of gaining attention. His research shows that we can only be conscious of one thing at a time (although we can switch around quickly among several items).

There is an internal filtering process between our sense organs and our consciousness. This is necessary because we can only process a limited amount of information at any moment. If it were not for this filtering, we would drown in a hopeless confusion of stimuli both from without and within.

Capture your listeners' attention.
Nothing happens unless you
first have their attention.

76

To communicate we must cut through the filter. Here are some helpful principles.

- Things that have been rewarding in the past are more likely to cut through the filter. That's why a child who can't hear her mother shouting at the top of her voice can hear the faint tinkle of an ice cream truck 20 blocks away!

- Things that signal danger get through. We become very aware of quiet footsteps following us in the dark.

- We tend to hear our names above the din. Addressing a student by name, for example, will usually end "wool gathering."

- Any sudden change in background (brighter, darker, louder, softer) gets our attention.

Broadbent also found that people can't sustain attention on any one thing very long. Even if they want to pay attention, their minds wander. This means we not only have to capture people's attention at the beginning of our message, but we also have to snag it again and again throughout our message.

Gratifying Listeners

Getting attention momentarily isn't the most difficult part. If you make a loud noise or whistle, you'll get people's attention involuntarily. But you can't hold it for more than a few seconds unless you give them some reason to continue to pay attention.

Give people a reason to pay attention by promising something they want or need.

An implied transaction takes place between a speaker and listeners. They will "sell" you their attention in exchange for

something of value which you will provide. The benefit you provide to your listeners can be either long-term (delayed gratification) or short-term (immediate gratification), or best of all, both.
Long-term, delayed gratification items could include:

- information listeners can use personally, such as, how to
  solve a problem they are experiencing. (A parent having
  trouble with a teenage son would listen carefully to someone who has been through the same experience and has
  found a successful outcome);

- information listeners can pass on to someone else, such as
  an important bit of news. This makes them feel valued because they can be the expert to someone else. (Many men
  read the sports page so they can have things to talk about
  with their sports fan friends. Or maybe they just don't
  want to seem dumb!)

Examples of short-term, immediate gratification items include:

- a joke;

- an interesting personal story;

- a picture of a baby, kitten, cute child, etc.;

- a sad story; (Perhaps surprisingly we like to hear about
  horrible and sad things as well as the pleasant and nice.);

- asking for information. (Most people find it rewarding to
  be able to help out someone in need and enjoy playing the
  expert.)

You must convey to listeners in the first few seconds some
sense of what it is you will give them. Here are some examples
of how you might do that.

- "Have you heard the story about? . . ." (Reward: a funny
  story, laughter.)

- "Did you hear what happened to? . . ." (Reward: information that can be repeated, satisfying curiosity.)

- "I was on my way to church last Sunday when. . . ." (Reward: a touching story, satisfying curiosity.)

- "Looks like you are having trouble with your ignition. . . ." (Reward: getting information to help solve an immediate problem.)

- "Preparing for the teenage years, next on AM Live." (Reward: getting information to help solve a long-term problem.)

- "Do you know anything about cars?" (Reward: getting to be the expert and to be helpful.)

- Sometimes you don't have to say anything; a smile is enough. (Reward: a possible friend.)

Increasing Your Chances of Being Heard

Communication scientist Wilbur Schramm[2] used the following formula to show the chances that a particular communication source would be selected:

$$\frac{\text{Promise of Reward}}{\text{Effort Required}} = \text{Probability of Selection}$$

From this you can see that reward and effort work against each other. A high reward with little effort leads to a high likelihood of selection, but a low reward with a large effort yields a small chance of being selected.

Make it easy for people to pay attention.

Obviously my message has a better chance of being selected if the effort required of listeners is low. How can I do this?

- Use easy-to-understand words and sentence construction, appropriate to the level of the audience.

- Be brief. Get to the point quickly.

- Include enough variety of presentation to hold attention well so the audience does not have to work hard to pay attention.

Remember that the potential listener or reader will decide to attend to your message based on the other choices she has available at the moment. I was at the airport late one evening and found that my wife's plane was to be two hours late! The newsstands were closed, and I had not brought anything to read. I managed to find a few pieces of an old newspaper and read almost every word even of sections I normally would not read.

Compare that to my present situation in our study at home. Here I have hundreds of books, periodicals, CDs, videotapes, papers, television channels, radio stations, etc., to choose from. In this case the probability of my selecting any one of them is small.

So, we must think about the competition for attention at any given moment. If we can catch people when they are bored for lack of communication, it won't be hard to capture their attention, but if they have many other attractive choices, it may be quite difficult. Unfortunately for the communicator, there are few times when most people are away from the plethora of media options that fill their lives.

Make your message more attractive than the competition. People have choices!

One way to hold attention is to limit the competition. We can do this for a brief period in such settings as a theater, a classroom, or a worship center. One of the reasons why motion pictures have more impact on the big screen than they do in video is because there are fewer distractions in the darkened theater than there are at home with kids, books, and magazines around, and especially the telephone!

Even when you have a more or less "captive audience" there are still plenty of distractions both from without and within. Think of the many times you have been at church, struggling to stay alert while the lesson or message seemed to drone on endlessly.

Filling the Mind

One reason why unaided speech can be so deadly dull is because it is *slow!* Consider that the average speaker says 120 to 150 words per minute. Even a relatively poor reader can read twice that speed, and a good reader can read 20 times that fast, or more. That means that something like 95 percent of the information processing capacity of the brain is unused when listening to speech.

Now add to this picture a slightly warm temperature and a bit of sleep deprivation during the past week, and the listener has a real problem. He *can't* stay awake! The speaker is not providing the minimum of mental stimulation needed to keep the audience awake and alert. The audience member must think about other things in order to avoid the embarrassment of going to sleep.

Give audience members something to think about or imagine to help keep their minds occupied so they won't start thinking about other things.

If the listener is filling her mind with things unrelated to the message, she will soon lose track of the message. How much better for the speaker to give her things to fill her mind. Here are some ideas.

- Use graphics related to the talk, especially photographs and charts with detail to be absorbed.

- Use "object lessons."

- Use drama or role-playing.

- Help the audience members use their imaginations. If you tell a story, they can imagine the details, making the experience more vivid in their minds.

Keeping It Interesting

When Rudolph Flesch[3] did some research to identify factors that make something interesting to read, he found one factor of great importance: the use of personal words and sentences. The more you use personal pronouns (I, we, you), personal names (like Sally, Fred, or Mr. Johnson), and tell personal stories, the more interesting your material will be.

Use personal words to make something seem interesting.

I think there are two reasons for this. First, we are interested in people. Perhaps even more important, we like stories. When I am using personal pronouns or names, I am probably telling a story about myself or some other person. I've noticed in my teaching if I'm lecturing about some abstract theoretical principles the class grows restless, but as soon as I start telling a story, I gain their rapt attention.

Why do we like stories? I think there are several reasons.

- We can use our imaginations, which makes the experience more vivid for us.

- A story usually contains some "twist," something unexpected. This builds our curiosity and gives us pleasure when that curiosity is satisfied.

- A story usually is organized along a time line, which is easy to follow.

- A story is usually told in simple language, easy to understand.

- A story is not theoretical or abstract, but concrete.

- A story is involving. We can see ourselves in the situation, which makes it powerful for us.

Tell stories to build and hold attention.

Because the audience likes stories, we may be tempted to tell stories simply for the sake of the pleasure they give. That's "entertainment." There is nothing wrong with entertainment if our goal is just to give momentary pleasure. If we plan to change behavior, however, we will need to learn to *use* stories to that end, as Jesus did.

Jesus the Storyteller

As a communicator, Jesus had a difficult assignment. He had to convince people to believe in a whole different realm of existence, fundamentally unlike anything they had experienced. Knowledge of that realm was crucial to his hearers because they had to make choices in this temporary form of existence that would determine their situation in the permanent realm.

Jesus knew the other realm well, having always existed there, so He didn't have to bone up on the subject matter to be communicated. The problem was how to present this profound information to creatures that had neither much capacity nor desire to learn. It's not that people were created dull, but they had already made harmful choices which greatly diminished their ability to think clearly.[4]

Jesus' parables often began, "The kingdom of heaven is like. . . ." Then would follow a simple story, involving familiar kinds of people or objects, something the listeners could easily imagine. By linking the unknown heavenly ideas to familiar earthly reality, He put divine truth within the grasp of mortals.

The principle is both simple and profound: create a link between what your listeners already know and what you wish them to know. Doing it isn't quite so easy. You have to know both what people know and don't know, then find something they do know that relates somehow to something they don't, and help them see the relationship. By using a story to bring the elements together, you have a better chance of capturing and holding the listener's interest.

We know that God chose many methods of communication over the years,[5] through the law and prophets for example, but the most effective communication was through His own Son, Jesus. Although fully God, Jesus was able to take the form of a man and live among us and eventually die for us.

Jesus' life was remarkable in two dimensions—His humanity and His divinity. God could have sent angels to hover over the ground and speak to the people. He could have written His message in the sky, or on golden plates, but He chose the medium of human flesh. He still does.

While Jesus' life was in many respects remarkably similar to the men and women around Him (so much so that some did not believe He was more than human), there were many clues to His divinity. These included His sinlessness, His unique wisdom, His selflessness. There were more spectacular signs: His miracles and His resurrection. His humanness made it possible for us to understand Him and to some extent made us willing to listen. His divine aspects demonstrated He was worth listening to!

Let your life tell a significant story.

Jesus often told stories, but His most important story was the one He lived. God has preserved that story, rich in detail, in the four Gospel accounts. What He did and what happened to Him are as important as the things He said. When we hear the story of Jesus, it comes with a sense of vividness and connectedness which abstract ideas cannot capture.

Most of the Old Testament heroes are more remarkable because of what they did rather than what they said. What Joseph or Daniel said, for example, takes on power when told in the context of their lives. Psalm 51, David's hymn of confession, takes on power when we know the *story* of his sin.[6]

Chapter Summary

Unless we capture listeners' attention, no communication takes place. Something unexpected may grab their attention for a moment, but then we must promise a reward for continued attention. The reward can be as simple as the pleasure of hearing a funny story, or getting information to help solve a problem. Stories are good for getting and maintaining attention because they are about people, are easy to follow, let us use our imagination, build curiosity, and contain an unexpected twist which gives pleasure.

1. Donald E. Broadbent, *Perception and Communication* (London: Pergamon Press, 1958).

2. Wilbur Schramm, *Men, Messages and Media: A Look at Human Communication* (New York: Harper and Row, 1973).

3. R.F. Flesch, "Marks of a Readable Style: A Study in Adult Education" (Ed.D. diss., Columbia University, New York, 1944).

4. See Romans 1:18-32.

5. See Hebrews 1:1-3.

6. See 2 Samuel 11.

CHAPTER FIVE

Become Attractive
to Your Audience

Psychologist H.C. Kellman[1] originated a helpful way of organizing the effects that a communication source can have. Using his terms, power leads to *compliance*, attractiveness leads to *identification*, and credibility leads to *internalization*. In this chapter we will consider attractiveness. We will consider what it means to be attractive, and the effect this has on the audience.

Attractiveness

A quick look around will convince you there is no universal standard of attractiveness. As my uncle Clyde put it when I sent him a picture of my bride-to-be, "What does a beautiful woman like her see in *you!*"

Attractiveness is largely a matter of personal preference or taste. When one of my students had a green mohawk, I had trouble seeing it as attractive, although I suppose his girlfriend did. On the other hand, now that I am middle-aged I see middle-aged women as attractive, which I suppose my student would have a hard time understanding. So we must think about attractiveness in relationship to a particular individual or group.

For whatever reasons, some people attract us, and when they do, we think of ourselves as being associated with them or similar to them in some regard. This is what Kellman calls, "identification."

The need to identify is blatantly expressed by children and teenagers. They often dress and behave like their TV heroes. Although the need becomes more subtle as we become adults, it is still there and is the basis of a great deal of advertising. A sports figure or an attractive woman basically says, "If you use the product I do, you can be like me!" Obviously that commercial has no power unless we are attracted to the personality.

In addition to physical attractiveness, researchers have studied three other components which are all strongly related to each other. These are: similarity, familiarity, and liking. If any one of these is true about your relationship with another, there is a good chance that all three will become true. For example, if you see someone as similar to yourself, you will want to spend time with that person, thus developing familiarity and liking.

Similarity

We are attracted to people who are like us.[2] We tend to like people of our own age group, educational level, religion, race, income level, location, and occupation. But similarity of ideas is even more important than these demographic factors. We are strongly attracted to people who have similar attitudes and opinions. The more opinions we hold in common, the stronger the attraction.

Emphasize the ways you are similar to your audience.

If others are to be attracted to you, they must see you as similar to themselves. You can help this process along by enhancing or pointing out similarities. If you are a bit older or younger than your audience, for example, you can dress more like they do to minimize the difference. In your introductory remarks you can let them know about values you share with them.

Years ago I was at a movie theater on an Army post in Okinawa to see a Youth for Christ team give a musical program. Unfortunately, no one had told the G.I.'s that there was to be a special program, so hundreds had come as they ordinarily did to see a movie. When the "religious" singing team came out instead, the crowd instantly became vocally hostile.

I gulped and prayed and saw a miracle. One of the team members started bantering with the audience in a lighthearted way and before long the young military men came to see YFC musicians as pretty much like themselves. They gave them a polite hearing and an enthusiastic response at the end.

Familiarity

The old saying, "Familiarity breeds contempt," seems only to be true at high levels of familiarity. Generally, research[3] shows the more we know someone the better we like him or her. We prefer people and topics that we have heard before.

That familiarity leads to liking is generally true of art forms as well as individuals. At the beginning of my five years in Japan, Japanese music sounded awful to me, but by the end of my stay I really liked it.

Of course we know from experience it is possible to get enough of a particular song (or food, or performer, etc.) so we don't want to hear it again for a while. When I was the program manager for a radio station, I learned that a new song would not be particularly well-liked by the audience until they heard it a few times. Then it rapidly climbed in popularity until after a while it had been heard so much the audience burned out on it. Then it had to be taken off for a while. I could reintroduce it later as a "golden oldie," but only play it occasionally.

I had to try to guess in advance which new songs had the potential of becoming hits. Best guesses? Those that were similar to recent hits, or by the same performers. We like the familiar.

Let people get to know you. They will like you better.

The choir director may not feel she is doing her job if she repeats anthems from time to time, but the congregation will probably like an anthem more the more often they hear it (up to a point).

Composers are aware of the benefit of familiarity. Many songs repeat the same fairly simple musical idea quite a number of times to build familiarity and liking. So that they can get the benefits of repetition without boredom setting in, they use a technique called, "variations on a theme"; the same basic theme is repeated, but with enough change so it doesn't get boring. Using variations, jazz musicians can sustain a simple melody for many minutes. Almost all popular and sacred music varies the key and often the voicing and rhythm during repeats.

Introduce some new elements when you are repeating things.

"Something old and something new. . . ." We like the familiar, but we also want some novelty. The familiar makes us feel comfortable and confident. The novel is exciting, but also dangerous. An effective communicator will provide just the right amount of each.

If you are a communicator who is new to the audience, use the familiar as much as you can in other things, such as clothing, settings, and music. You could also make yourself familiar (and thus liked) through media exposure, such as radio, television, cable, and newspapers. You should "borrow" familiarity by quoting familiar authors, using familiar music, etc., in your communication.

Liking

It comes as no surprise that we are attracted to communicators we like. How do you become liked? Research shows that familiarity and similarity lead to liking. On the other hand, if we like a person, we tend to see her as more similar and familiar than she really is!

We also like communicators who reward us. According to researchers Berscheid and Walster,[4] communicators can reward us in the following ways:

- reduction of anxiety, stress, loneliness, or insecurity. This can be in the form of comfort, reassurance, or diversion;

- social approval. Show the receiver you like him/her and/or show the person how to be liked by others;

- proximity. We like people better if we are physically close to them. One-to-one and small group settings are more effective than large groups. Mass media communication should usually be produced to give a sensation of closeness;

- cooperation. We like people who help us reach our goals, and we don't like people who frustrate us.

Reward your listeners.

Cognitive Dissonance

The theory of "Cognitive Dissonance" presented by Dr. Leon Festinger at Stanford[5] is one of a fascinating group of theories called "balance theories." The basic idea is simple. Just as there are clashing colors and dissonant musical notes, there are also thoughts which, when held together in the mind at the same time, cause a kind of mental clash or dissonance. According to Festinger, when we experience this mental unpleasantness, we will be motivated to change something to make it go away.

For example, let's suppose that you, a Christian, have a close friend who is Islamic. Other than religion you have a lot in common, and a cordial friendship has developed over time. You have been reluctant to say anything about your faith because you do not want to offend your friend, but you are experiencing some *dissonance* because you care about your friend's eternal destination. So one evening you invite him over, open your heart, and disclose deeply about your faith. He doesn't say much at the time, and he hasn't returned your phone calls since. He, too, is experiencing dissonance. He probably has three conflicting thoughts: (1) he values you as a friend, (2) you are a Christian, (3) he has no respect for Christians.

If he can change any one of those thoughts, he can restore harmony to his thinking. He can: (1) devalue you as a friend, (2) pretend you are not a Christian or that religion isn't important (which is hard now that you have confronted him), or (3) change his ideas about Christians.

Build a strong friendship as a basis for sharing the Gospel. If the person is antagonistic to the Truth, don't say too much too soon.

Which will he do? Unfortunately it's hard to predict. If he values your friendship more than he values his attitude about

Christians, he will probably come to see Christians as less bad than he originally thought. On the other hand, if he holds strongly to his opinion about Christians, he will probably give up or devalue his friendship with you. He may do some of each.

What can you do in a situation like this?

- Build strong friendships. Invest time and effort in the other person. The stronger the friendship, the more resistant it is to being devalued.

- Don't be too quick to present too much of the Gospel. Let the persuasion process be gradual over time.

- Try not to be confrontational. Don't deny the importance of the Gospel to you, but try to be natural and friendly in your presentation.

- Don't avoid presenting the Gospel for fear of offending. It is better to offend than to never present the truth. But if the truth can be presented in an inoffensive way, all the better.

Physical Attractiveness

Does physical attractiveness make any difference in how persuasive a person is? Research implies that it does.[6] Studies show that physically attractive people are thought to be more liked, more likely to succeed, better workers, stronger, more sensitive, and even more modest. While we must remember that God looks on the heart, humans can only look on the outside so we do need to give outward appearance some attention!

Take reasonable measures to enhance your physical attractiveness by careful grooming and appropriate clothing choices. Attractive people are more effective communicators.

What are the implications for the communicator?

- If you are considering a media ministry, make a realistic appraisal of whether your speaker's appearance will enhance or detract from the program. Some people have a great face for radio!

- Make the most of what you've got. If you have a public ministry where appearance is important, get good advice about hairstyle and clothing.[7] Many physical defects can be covered, disguised, or minimized by appropriate hairstyling and clothing.

- If you have physical features that are definitely distracting (such as protruding ears or a prominent wart), consider having them surgically fixed.

- Be careful in your personal grooming. A careless disregard for appearance will make you a less effective communicator.

- Remember that the purpose of improving your appearance is not for personal aggrandizement or to become sexually provocative. It is to be seen as a more attractive communicator of God's message. Avoid clothing styles that communicate the wrong message.

- Don't lose perspective. What you say and how you say it is much more important than physical appearance. Some of the most effective speakers are not very good-looking. The Apostle Paul was apparently physically disfigured.

Chapter Summary

An attractive communicator will be more likely to gain a hearing. People will listen and perhaps adopt new ideas because they want to be associated in some way with the speaker. Attractive ideas are more important than an attractive body, but an appealing body helps too. People in the audience are more likely to view you as attractive if you are similar (especially in values) to them, and if they are familiar with you. The more they like you the more they will believe you. If the audience should change its opinion about your attractiveness, they will also discard what you say, unless by that time they have come to accept the message on its own merit.

1. H.C. Kelman, "Processes of Opinion Change," *Public Opinion Quarterly* 25 (1961): 54–78.

2. A good general discussion of the research findings can be found in: Alexis S. Tan, *Mass Communication Theories and Research*, 2nd ed. (New York: John Wiley and Sons, 1985), 116–41.

3. Adapted from William McGuire, "The Nature of Attitudes and Attitude Change," in G. Lindzey and E. Aronson, eds., *The Handbook of Social Psychology*, 2nd ed., (Reading, Mass.: Addison-Welsey, 1969), vol. 3, 177–99.

4. Ellen Berscheid and Elaine Walster, *Interpersonal Attraction* (Reading, Mass.: Addison-Wesley, 1969).

5. Leon Festinger, "The Theory of Cognitive Dissonance," in *The Science of Human Communication*, ed. Wilbur Schramm (New York: Basic Books, 1963).

6. For a discussion of the literature, see: Alexis S. Tan, *Mass Communication Theories and Research*, 2nd ed. (New York: John Wiley and Sons, 1985).

7. Though it's now a bit dated, John Molloy's book *Dress for Success* has many valuable tips.

CHAPTER SIX

Develop Credibility

J esus had a serious credibility problem, and so do we! In appearance and speech He was similar to other men of His day, yet He claimed to be Almighty God. Though people knew He was born to the village carpenter's wife, He claimed to have always existed.

So sincere seekers would not miss Him, God gave His Son credentials. These included the many prophecies He fulfilled even in things beyond His control, such as the manner of His birth and death. His miracles convinced some although many people saw them simply as entertainment or a way to get free food. His ability to give remarkable answers to loaded questions won over some. His sacrificial lifestyle and death gave credence to His words, and the astounding miracle of His resurrection authenticated His credentials to all who were not willingly blind.

As Christians today, we too have a credibility problem. We who claim to be powered by the very Spirit of God often live no differently than those around us. As Jesus did, we can take steps to maximize our effectiveness.

Why Should Anyone Listen to You?

A large body of research shows that we are influenced by *who* says something. In a typical study identical messages are given to two similar groups. One group is told that the message comes from a well-respected expert in the field, and the other group is told the message comes from someone like a college sophomore, or other non-expert. After members read messages, the attitudes of the two groups is measured. Typically the group who thought the message was coming from an expert found it more believable.

What factors make a person more believable or credible? Researchers Berlo, Lemert, and Mertz[1] did a large study and came up with three main factors. They called these factors *safety, qualification,* and *dynamism.* Other researchers have used different terms, but most agree on the nature of the first two factors.

Let people know you have nothing to gain personally from influencing them. They will be more likely to believe you.

The *safety* factor has to do with trustworthiness, or what some researchers have called disinterestedness. The idea is that you can trust the speaker not to lead you knowingly astray. Being "disinterested" means that the source has nothing to gain (no self-interest) in lying, so is more likely to tell the truth. We would be more likely to trust a salesperson who was not on commission, for example.

The *qualification* dimension is often called "expertise," and has to do with the source's competence or training in the subject at hand. Terms that would describe a highly qualified person might include: *trained, experienced, skillful, informed, authoritative, able,* and *intelligent.*[2]

Introduce a speaker in such a way that people understand his or her expertise.

The third factor, *dynamism* (amount of energy), is not as important as the first two and is not mentioned at all by some researchers. Erwin Bettinghaus in his excellent summary discusses a category he calls "personal characteristics."[3] These factors are more powerful when the receiver has little other basis for forming an opinion about the source. When we don't know a speaker, we are more likely to be affected by hesitations, apparent lack of confidence, and the like.

It's important to remember that credibility does not depend entirely on the characteristics of the source, but also on the *receiver's perceptions* of the source. Proverbs says even a fool will be thought wise if he keeps silent.[4] From this we can guess that an unknown person is granted a moderate level of credibility by the receiver, which he can either build on and increase, or which he can destroy if he, like the fool, opens his mouth and displays his ignorance.

A source who is credible to one receiver may not be to another. When I was doing some research for a film with speaker Josh McDowell in the 1970s, I was surprised that he spoke to large college audiences while wearing well-worn jeans and very casual shirts. I came to realize that for this audience and time such clothing would actually increase his credibility, while for older audiences it would severely diminish his credibility.

Which factors are most important in determining a speaker's credibility? Of course that depends on the receiver and the topic, but researcher Judy Burgoon reviewed the literature and summed it up this way: "The ideal source would be highly (i.e., near the extreme) responsible, reliable, honest, just, kind, cooperative, nice, pleasant, sociable, cheerful, friendly, good-natured, and relaxed and only slightly (i.e., near neutral) expert, virtuous, refined, calm, composed, verbal, mild, extroverted, bold, and talkative."[5]

Don't overemphasize your qualifications. It is possible to be too much of an expert!

In general our credibility increases according to our strengths in the areas of trustworthiness or safety (responsibility, reliability, honesty, justice). It is possible, however, to be too extreme in qualifications (expert) and personal characteristics (refined, calm, composed, verbal, mild, extroverted, bold, and talkative).

Increasing Credibility

Here are some practical suggestions as to how you can increase your credibility.

■ Be trustworthy. No flimflam. Do what you say you will do. Pay your bills on time, meet your obligations. Let your yes be yes, and your no, no.[6] Word gets around when you say one thing and do another.

I am embarrassed to tell you that as a young Christian called into missions I left Albany, Oregon without paying a hospital bill that was past due. (Of course I intended to pay it eventually.) Since I had been an announcer on a Christian radio station, my testimony was known. Even so, I was surprised to receive an angry note from the hospital administrator telling me that what I was doing was a terrible testimony.

She was right of course. Even though I was embarrassed, I became very grateful for her rebuke. I quickly sold a piano my grandmother had given me and paid the bill. That was the right thing to do, only I should have done it sooner!

- Emphasize similarity. Just as we like people similar to ourselves, we also trust them more. Sociologist Everett Rogers found that the more a source and receiver have in common (he calls this "homophily") the more the receiver will change his or her behavior to agree with the source.[7] Your audience may see themselves as being more different from you than you see yourself as being different from them. You will need to find and highlight common elements in your lives if you are to be trusted. You could also do things with your receivers so you have shared experiences.

- Use status. The way society is organized, some positions or occupations have higher status than others. Those in higher status positions are generally given more credibility by virtue of the position. Status is relative to that of the audience members and their perceptions.

    This brings about a dilemma. In Christ every part of the body is equal,[8] and we are told not to think of ourselves more highly than we ought.[9] Still, some people have experiences or positions that make them more attractive. These credentials need to somehow be communicated for the benefit of the hearers. This is often done during a speaker's introduction or on the dust jacket of a book. Such information should be factual and not puffed up.

- Increase your expertise. People who are sought for their knowledge are more likely to read specialized journals, attend seminars, take courses, travel, and talk to experts. However, if you are already perceived as an expert (for example, a pastor would be seen as an expert in theology), you will gain little additional credibility by expanding your knowledge (for example: getting a higher degree). Moderate values of perceived expertise are most effective.

> **Ethical Point**
> Don't exaggerate or lie about your qualifications as an information source.

Borrowing Credibility

If you have little credibility with a particular audience, perhaps because you are not known, you can "borrow" some by making reference to high credibility people or institutions.

Use other people's credibility.
If people don't know or trust you,
quote others whom they do know and trust.

- Ask for an introductory letter. When I was beginning "deputation" (raising support) as a new Far East Broadcasting Company missionary, my pastor, who was highly respected in his denomination, sent out a letter of introduction on my behalf. His letter produced speaking engagements for me in several churches. Without his letter I might never have made it as a missionary.

  It might be that a person who knows and trusts you is not up-to-date on your qualifications. Give her a current résumé, or even a suggested letter that she could send. As a professor I am frequently called upon to write reference letters, and I always appreciate being reminded of the former student's experience, academic standing, and any honors.

- Ask for an introduction. Ask someone to personally introduce you who is known and trusted by the individual you wish to influence.

  If you are speaking before a church group, it is especially important to have the pastor introduce you. Give the pastor some biographical information so he can do this well. My own experience as a missionary doing fund-raising was that I rarely received support from a church when the pastor was not there as I spoke.

- Ask for a "to whom it may concern" letter. This is a letter written about you which can be shown (or a copy given) to those you wish to influence. The higher the credibility of the writer the better.

- Use a board of reference. Many organizations list a "board of reference" on their letterhead. If I don't know an organization, I frequently scan the board of reference to see if there are any names I know and trust. If I recognize one name, I am much more likely to trust the organization.

  In setting up a board of reference, you should seek well-known and highly credible people. Ideally, you should have at least one name that would be known and trusted by every denomination, constituency, or group with whom you hope to deal.

- List references. If you are known to people who would be known and trusted by your receivers, list these names (with their permission, of course).

- Drop names. We've all been irritated with people who try to impress us by "dropping" the names of well-known people into their conversations, as if they are on a first-name basis with these people; however, if you do know a person who would be trusted by the audience and you can do so in an honest and unpretentious way, use the name.

- Mention categories. Sometimes it isn't so important that you know a specific person as that you know people of a category. For example, if you are speaking to farmers, you would increase your credibility if you had spent any time on a farm, had spoken to farm groups, knew prominent farmers, or knew any farmers at all!

- Quote trusted sources. If you are unknown, salt your communication liberally with quotes, references, and statistics from well-known and trusted individuals and institutions. To gain the benefit of borrowed credibility, be

101

sure to give the author's name, and if the name isn't well known, give the author's position or affiliation. If the person is quoted in a trusted publication, give the name of the publication. You could say, for example, "*Time* magazine quoted UCLA psychologist Dr. John Blank as saying. . . ." This way you gain the credibility of *Time*, UCLA, the fact that the person has a doctorate, and the content of the actual quote.

Borrowing Credibility from God

We who are God's agents in the world have the right and responsibility to speak for Him. When we speak in God's name, we are borrowing some of His credibility. If people think we are giving God's message, they will tend to believe it and act on it; therefore, we have a heavy moral responsibility to be careful how we represent God.

Speak boldly but carefully when you speak for God.

I once worked for a man who often said, "God told me" to do whatever it was he was doing. The man was an earnest and sincere Christian, and I believe he actually thought God had directed him to do these things, but I also think he was *wrong* some of the time. Quite a number of the things God supposedly told him to do proved to be mistakes which had to be abandoned or corrected.

In the same way, several prominent television evangelists have raised large amounts of money for projects they claimed God was telling them to do. Many of these projects have been abandoned. This is a serious problem. When we say we are speaking for God and what we say doesn't prove to be true, we certainly undermine our credibility, and in the eyes of many we may undermine God's credibility. We certainly don't want others to speak evil of God because of us!

In Old Testament times false prophets were to be executed![10] Their words had to square with Scripture and had to come to pass as they predicted. In our day of very little accountability, people use "God told me. . . ." glibly. But Scripture says God cares greatly about the use of His name and the integrity of His Word.[11] Teachers are warned that we are subject to a stricter judgment.[12]

It's tempting to claim our thoughts and words are from God. It ends arguments. It's hard to disagree with someone who says, "God told me" to do this or that. These words also imply that the speaker has a special status, being one to whom the Lord speaks face-to-face as He did with Moses.

In saying this I don't mean to suggest that God is silent today. I believe He has spoken to me on some occasions. But I also believe we can confuse our own thoughts, desires, fantasies, and dreams with God's voice. I remember once when I was leaving home through the back door, I had a strong impression that I should check the front door, and sure enough it was unlocked! Thank you, Lord. But other times I have also had strong impressions to do things which did not work out. If I took these urges or impressions to be always the voice of God, I would be wrong much of the time!

> **Ethical Point**
> Don't say, "God told me. . . ." carelessly. Those who purport to speak in the name of God must be certain they are speaking His message. To use the name of God to enhance our own messages is as clear a violation of the third commandment as is cursing!

The saddest thing is to hear people claim God led them to do things that are clearly contradictory to Scripture. I heard of a pastor who entered into an adulterous relationship with a woman from his congregation and claimed that God supernaturally brought them together! Such is the power of satanic- and self-deception.

How can we speak confidently as God's agents without misrepresenting Him?

- Use Scripture, correctly interpreted and applied. I believe much of Billy Graham's effectiveness comes from his frequent use of the phrase, "The Bible says. . . ." We must always be careful because even Scripture can be twisted and incorrectly applied.

- Recognize the Bible as the highest authority. If you believe God has spoken to you or is leading you in a particular direction, make sure that direction is fully in agreement with the teaching of the Bible. You could be confused or deceived about what you take to be God's voice.

- Qualify your statements. If you believe God is leading you, say something like, "I believe God is leading me. . . ." or, "I feel strongly this is what God wants us to do." Don't say, "God told me. . . ." Your words will still make a powerful and confident statement, yet allow for the *possibility* of being wrong.

- Be humble. You have been wrong before and you will be again. Be careful not to confuse your thoughts with those of the One who said: "For my thoughts are not your thoughts, neither are your ways my ways. . . . As the heavens are higher than the earth, so are my ways higher than your ways and my thoughts than your thoughts."[13]

Chapter Summary

People will be more inclined to believe and act on what you tell them if they see you as being knowledgeable and trustworthy. You will seem more trustworthy if you don't have anything to gain personally by convincing other people.

You can enhance the audience's understanding of your expertise by asking someone to mention your qualifications during the introduction. You can also "borrow" credibility by referring to known and trusted sources.

When "borrowing credibility" from God, be careful not to go beyond what God actually says so as not to bring discredit upon yourself or God.

1. D.K. Berlo, J.B. Lemert, and R.J. Mertz, "Dimensions for Evaluating the Acceptability of Message Sources" (Research Monograph, Department of Communication, Michigan State University, 1966).

2. The list is from Erwin P. Bettinghaus, *Persuasive Communication*, 3rd ed. (New York: Holt, Rinehart, and Winston, 1980), 93. This book contains an excellent discussion of the entire area of credibility.

3. Ibid.

4. Proverbs 17:28.

5. J. Burgoon, "Ideal Source Credibility: A Reexamination of Source Credibility Measurement," *Central States Speech Journal*, vol. 27, (1976), 200–6.

6. See James 5:12.

7. Everett M. Rogers and F. Floyd Shoemaker, *Communication of Innovations*, 2nd ed. (New York: Free Press, 1971), 240–43.

8. See 1 Corinthians 12.

9. See Romans 12:3.

10. See Deuteronomy 13 and Jeremiah 28 for example.

11. See Revelation 22:18-19 and Exodus 20:1-7.

12. See James 3:1.

13. See Isaiah 55:8. See also Psalm 94:11.

Make Yourself Heard

Choose Appropriate Media

What is a *medium*?
A medium is something that goes between and suspends, holds, or carries something else. For example,
the medium for an artist might be acrylic paints. In this case the
acrylic material suspends or carries the pigments which is the
part you see. Because we are not able to directly inject our
thoughts into another person's mind, we must convey them
using symbols carried by a medium. As you read my words, the
medium is paper and ink.

Actually, the book in your hands is just one link in a complex
chain of *media* (plural for medium) which starts with thoughts
in my mind and ends with thoughts in your mind. My thoughts
are translated into words, which then are transformed into finger movements which operate the keyboard of my computer.
The electronic images are eventually stored on a magnetic disk,
which (after much editing) is transformed into the printing
plates for the book. The printing press reproduces the pattern
of the words by applying ink to the paper. Finally, this pattern
is reflected by light to your eyes, then conveyed by your nerves

to your brain where it is decoded into some approximation of my original thoughts.

We think of radio, television, film, and newspapers as media. This is really a shortening of the proper term, *mass media.* You cannot communicate at all without some form of medium. Even in face-to-face communication the air which carries the sound waves and the reflected light which carries the visual images are media. The form of communication which is the least mediated is touching. Even here the touch sensors in the skin and the nervous system serve as media to carry the message to the brain.

Media choices are influenced by many factors, some of which are indicated in the following chart.

Factors Influencing Media Choices

Medium	Size of Group			
	One	Small Group	Large Group	Mass Audience
Face-to-face	Highly effective	Very effective	Fairly effective	Not practical for most purposes
Motion Picture		Effective but costly	Very effective, moderate cost	Very effective, moderate cost
Broadcast TV		Probably not practical	Probably not practical	Effective and efficient
Videotape	Effective, but costly	Effective, moderate cost	Effective, low cost	Effective, but expensive compared to broadcast television

| Medium | Size of Group | | | |
	One	Small Group	Large Group	Mass Audience
Radio			Probably not practical	Effective at persuasion, less effective at conveying information, very cost efficient
Telephone	Effective at persuasion, less effective at conveying information	Less costly but less effective than face-to-face		
Newspaper/ magazine				Effective for certain audiences, relatively high cost
Letter	Effective at conveying information, less effective at persuasion. Moderate cost	Moderate effectiveness, moderate cost	Moderate effectiveness, moderate cost	Relative to mass media can be more effective, but is much more costly

Face-to-Face Media Choices

In face-to-face situations the media are usually air and light. These media offer you many choices. You can speak certain words, use a particular tone of voice, write a note, gesture, nod or shake your head, move your body, look the person in the eye, dress in a particular way, show up promptly, or show emotion on your face. I could also combine these.

Your choices of media greatly impact your effectiveness. The following chart will help you make good choices.

111

Choices for Face-to-Face, One-to-One Communication

Message Mode	Advantages	Disadvantages
Spoken words (word choice)	Efficiently conveys thoughts, fairly precise, wide range of meaning possible	May be misunderstood, does not convey feelings as effectively as thoughts
Tone of voice (includes factors such as, pitch changes, rate of speaking, distinctness, and loudness)	Effectively conveys feelings, emotions Gives information about how to interpret accompanying words	Ineffectively conveys thoughts Meaning often not very precise Easy to misunderstand
Gestures (hand movements)	Can emphasize or illustrate spoken words, and in some cases has wordlike meaning Gives information about how to interpret accompanying words	Except in a few cases ineffective at conveying thoughts
Eye contact	Direct contact communicates honesty and directness Looking away as you pause in your speech indicates an incomplete thought	Darting eyes and indirect eye contact communicate nervousness and probably dishonesty
Posture (erect, leaning forward, slouching, leaning back, etc.)	Indicates relative interest and energy or state of relaxation of speaker	Easy for speaker to give off unwanted cues Leaning back to mask personal nervousness may appear as low energy or lack of interest
Proximity (how close you are to the other person)	Can make the message more personal and powerful	May be frightening and too intense, therefore causing strong negative reaction Appropriate distance is culturally related
Photographs or drawings (sketches done during talk or prepared earlier and brought out during talk)	Can communicate much more easily than words Can help to hold interest	May distract from spoken words

Message Mode	Advantages	Disadvantages
Word graphics	Can emphasize points, make them memorable, offer structure, and bridge points	May interfere with spoken words
Touching (handshake, embrace, etc.)	Can be very powerful to show caring, warmth, genuineness	Can stir emotions that may be misunderstood
Dress	Helps to define the situation as formal, informal, etc., and to define the speaker as one who should be taken seriously	Easily misunderstood Someone who dresses as "casual" can be seen as sloppy
Jewelry	Can have specific meaning such as being married or engaged or being Christian or Jewish or gay Can be seen as making the person more attractive	Can be easily misunderstood, especially earrings in males Can also look cheap and garish
Makeup	May make the person seem more vivid and even normal	May cause speaker to appear strange or cheap may cause men to be seen as vain or effeminate
Hairstyle	Can communicate such things as being competent versus being cute or rebellious	Deviant style may make the communicator less effective
Cleanliness and grooming	A clean, well-groomed communicator will be more effective except in situations where a worker would be expected to be dirty (such as a farm, mine, or oil field)	Unkempt hair, spots on clothing, etc., will detract from your effectiveness, and may even make you repulsive to the hearer
Taste (serving food or drink)	May make the message more effective	May be costly or inconvenient
Scents (perfumes, colognes, aftershaves, body odor, etc.)	May enhance the communication, while an unpleasant one will detract. No discernible scent at all is considered the standard for business.	May be interpreted incorrectly as an attempt to seem sexy May seem unpleasant too some people May invoke allergies in some people

One-on-one, face-to-face communication is considered the most powerful and persuasive form, and I think the reason can be understood from the chart above. Every sense organ or channel to the brain can be used. There are also social expectations in a face-to-face situation that make it awkward for a person not to pay attention. In addition many kinds of feedback (posture, eye behavior, and facial expressions) can let you know if the receiver understands and agrees with what you are saying, even without explicit verbal feedback.

Use face-to-face communication when time and money permit because it is usually the most powerful form of communication.

Face-to-face, one-to-one communication does have some disadvantages. First, it's expensive! It requires your time and the receiver's time, and it often requires travel. It requires a suitable place (such as a restaurant) and you must groom and dress appropriately. If you had to reach a million people, face-to-face, one-to-one communication would be impossible.

Face-to-face may be too intense for some situations. A guy would be unlikely to go to a girl's house to ask for a first date. That would seem too pushy and inappropriate. Instead he would telephone her.

Mass Media Choices

As we move away from a face-to-face situation, something electronic or mechanical comes between the source and receiver. We lose fidelity in some aspects of communication, and we lose other aspects altogether. The narrowest channel is print. Here we get only words, and lose the voice qualities, gestures, appearance, eye contact, posture, clothing, jewelry, grooming, and scent of the speaker. Because we use many of these nonverbal aspects of communication to help us judge sincerity, we may be less willing to trust print. If a speaker, however, comes across as insincere in person, he might do better in print!

Use print for complicated material and if you tend to come across as insincere in person.

Radio is a broader channel than print because in addition to the words you have the other vocal qualities that help you trust and interpret the words. The telephone gives you the words and vocal qualities in poor fidelity but adds the enormous advantage of being two-way so you can receive immediate feedback.

Use radio. Generally people trust radio more than print because the tone of voice helps them judge the speaker's credibility.

The least restrictive mass medium is film (if you are most concerned about quality of picture) or television (if you are most concerned about immediacy). With both film and television you have words, vocal qualities, eye behavior, posture, appearance, dress, etc. You only miss the ability to be physically touched, and to smell the speaker. Of course the sound and picture are not the same quality as if you were really there, and feedback is difficult and slow. If you add a telephone circuit for immediate feedback (as you have in some classroom television situations), you have a very strong system.

Use film and television. They are the least restrictive channels. Visual elements, however, may distract from the words and vice versa.

Some have attempted to add the "smell" channel to motion pictures, but so far they have failed. Difficulties include a vast array of scents, any of which need to be delivered instantly, then just as quickly disappear. You can see that the air-handling problems would be enormous.

I had a little experience with "smell-a-vision" myself. In high school we were doing a play set in a swamp. We asked the chemistry teacher if he could come up with something that would smell like a swamp. He did, and it was somewhat convincing when whiffed briefly.

On the night of the play we poured quantities of the chemical into shallow containers placed around the auditorium. Before long the entire auditorium was awash with the most vile smell. People were looking at their neighbors, wondering "who did it." We finally had to stop the play (by now you couldn't hear it anyway), apologize, pick up the scent containers, and air out the auditorium before we could continue. I've never had a desire to experiment with scents again!

Media That Transcend Time

When Joshua led the Children of Israel into the Promised Land, God gave them a dramatic visual illustration of His great power and faithfulness. He heaped up the Jordan river, and took them across on dry land. That surely must have impressed them!

But God knew they wouldn't remember it for long, so He used two long-lasting media to help them remember. The first was two heaps of stones, one on the shore and the other in the water. The second long-lasting medium came a little later but lasted longer—the written account found in Joshua chapters 3 and 4. God caused a dramatic but fleeting moment to be record-ed in a material (physical) form so that the account would continue to exist through the ages.

I once had tickets for a play, but forgot about them. When I found the unused tickets, I called the theater to ask if I could get a refund. I was reminded, "There is nothing more perishable than a theater ticket." Of course! The play had gone on in front of my empty, reserved seats, even though I was not there to see it.

Some media, such as television newscasts, are like that. They exist only in a limited time span, then are gone forever. These are media that come to you in the form of energy, whether electrical or sound waves. Unless these waves are captured in some material form (such as recording tape or film), they disappear.

A personal interview or a theatrical performance has a large impact on us at the time, but may be quickly forgotten, whereas a book may be around for years, at the ready any time we wish to refer to it.

Team media that are quickly forgotten with those that are permanently recorded.

A good technique is to team the two kinds of media: those that have a large impact but exist only in a short period of time with those which exist over longer periods of time.

- Follow a phone call or personal visit with a letter or fax, containing a summary of the decisions made and who is going to do what.

■ Offer a cassette tape of your church's services. (Note: If you include music or other copyrighted material, you will need to get permission to record it, and you will have to pay a royalty.)

■ Make printed material concerning your church or ministry available to visitors or listeners.

■ Offer a printed transcript, audio tape, or video recording of television or radio broadcasts.

Media That Transcend Space

My grandfather was a student of prophecy, and he liked to talk about the end times. One thing I puzzled over as a child was how people from the entire world[1] could see the bodies of the "two witnesses." Now it seems obvious — television. With more than 1 billion sets worldwide (for about 5.5 billion people), the majority of people in the world have access to a set. Television coverage is growing rapidly, jumping 50 percent in the past five years. Satellite "footprints" cover most of the earth. Only about half of Mexican homes have telephones, but virtually all have TV sets. Thai consumers buy TV sets before fans or refrigerators.[2]

In the near future more powerful satellites and video compression techniques will make many more channels available worldwide.

When Lech Walesa was asked what had brought about the end of Communism in Poland, he pointed toward a television set. Broadcasting has literally caused not only political revolutions, but also revolutions of morals and styles. American popular culture is known worldwide. As the *Los Angeles Times* put it, "Madonna writhes on MTV videos from Bahrain to Bangladesh."

My grandfather helped me learn about broadcasting in another way. As a homesteader, he farmed in simple, old-fashioned ways, which included "broadcasting" the seed onto the field. Broadcasting simply means *to cast (throw) broadly.* He would walk over the fields in a systematic way, throwing out seed. The idea of sending out messages broadly for anyone to pick up was a new one in the early days of broadcasting, so the analogy of a farmer spreading seed was a good one.

Broadcasting has many advantages which you can put to good use.

- The messages can go to places you can't — both geographically and socially. Far Eastern Broadcasting Company found many Catholic priests who, at that time, were forbidden to enter a Protestant church, but did listen to Protestant programming.

- Broadcasting has power to overcome selectivity. You can't "fast forward" or skip over material that is coming to you in real time, so you tend to listen through things you would otherwise avoid just to hear what's coming next. A short, Christian message placed as a commercial on a secular radio station will reach many more non-Christians than a half-hour broadcast on a Christian station. Broadcasting has power to deliver a message to people who are not seeking it.

- Broadcasting is timely. The signal gets to us at the speed of light — essentially instantaneously. Broadcast news tells us what is happening now, not what happened yesterday.

- Broadcasting is cheap! Since broadcast signals are transmitted from the producer to the receiver by means of radio waves and do not require production or transportation of a material medium (such as paper or videotape) the cost is just a fraction of other media on a per-receiver basis.

Use short, Christian messages on secular radio or television stations to reach nonbelievers.

Patterns of Media Use

We habitually use various forms of media, based in part on the medium's suitability for our purpose. Other factors also influence these choices, including economics and habits. Some needs and the media we habitually turn to are listed below.

- The need to know what's happening. For up-to-date information on current events the preferred media are television and radio. Sometimes a matter is of so little importance that it is not carried in broadcasting, or is of such importance that people tell strangers about it (as in the case of Kennedy's assassination). But for most ordinary information we hear it first through broadcasting.

- The need for more in-depth information, perspective, or analysis. For these we turn to newspapers and news magazines such as *Time* or *U.S. News and World Report,* a few broadcast news analysis programs, and nonfiction books.

- The need for specialized or technical information. For this we probably turn to specialized "niche" magazines, such as *PC Magazine* for computer buffs, or *Popular Photography* for photo buffs, or technical journals, such as the *Journal of the American Medical Association,* or to specialized nonfiction books, such as this one.

- The need for pleasure and escape. For this we use motion pictures, television, and fiction books. It is largely this need that drives the entertainment industry and motivates the average viewer in the U.S. to watch almost four hours of television daily.

  Most people decide first to watch television or go to the movies, then select among the available offerings in that time frame, choosing the "least objectionable program" of those available. Entertainment can make the problems of the world seem to recede for a while, so in this sense it can be compared to a drug, and can be addictive.

- To pass time, eliminate boredom and loneliness. Any medium can fill this function, but television is used most often. Households sometimes use television as a clock,
"You know you have to leave for school before the second commercial." A single friend of mine keeps her television set on all night long. When she wakes up during the
night she can tell what time it is by what program is on,
and she has a sense of companionship.

Matching Media and Message

Messages can be encoded through several means, such as,
words, tone of voice, gestures and body movements, pictures,
diagrams and charts, music, color, and motion. Media vary in
their ability to present these media messages.

Use print to effectively
communicate complex ideas.

- Print is best for words alone (without tone of voice, gestures, and body movements) and for still pictures. Because we can read about five times faster than we can listen, print is very time-effective in getting ideas across.
With print we set our own pace so we can skip parts we
don't need and repeat parts we don't understand. Not
surprisingly then, research shows we *learn* best from
print. Print is also excellent for still pictures, charts, and
graphs.

- Audio alone (radio or audio tapes) combines several advantages. It is excellent for speech and music where the
visual channel would contribute little additional information, or perhaps even distract. Some well-known authors
and radio speakers have an appearance or mannerisms

121

which would make them less effective on television than they are on radio. We *trust* someone we hear more because we can judge his sincerity and intensity by the tone of his voice. Audio is also much cheaper to produce and broadcast than video.

Use radio or audio tape when trust is important but pictures are not needed. It is inexpensive.

■ Video, film, or television. These media are best for capturing attention, creating excitement, and allowing for gestures, posture, movement, facial expression, and color. Video and film are expensive to produce, but in many cases they are able to attract such large audiences that the cost per viewer may be competitive. Video and film are most effective at persuasion, especially when emotional factors and such things as movement and color are important.

Use film and video. They are the most persuasive and powerful media, but also the most expensive.

Chapter Summary

In a sense all communication is mediated because I can't directly inject my thoughts into your mind. My thoughts must instead travel by media such as air, light, paper, or ink. When we are face-to-face with another individual, we have the most channels of communication available plus the power of social expectations that the person will at least pretend to pay attention.

One-to-one communication is the most powerful medium but also the most expensive. For example, you paid only a few dollars for this book, much less than it would cost for me to travel to your home and personally tell you everything it says. For the sake of greater economy or convenience, we choose mass media. We need to find a good match between a particular medium's features and the requirements for a communication situation. Film and television are the least restrictive media, print the most. Print, however, is often best for communication of complicated ideas, such as those in this book!

Some media, such as books, transcend time. Others, such as television, can transcend long distances almost instantaneously. We use media in habitual ways. For example, we may use motion pictures primarily for entertainment and newspapers primarily for information. We trust radio and television more because they better convey the nonverbal aspects of communication.

An Additional Thought

This chapter has been about how you as a communicator can choose media to most effectively deliver your message; however, I think it is also appropriate to include a word of caution about the ways most of us consume the media. I am concerned that most Christians have no more discernment about their media use than non-Christians do. We somehow imagine that we are immune to the sex and violence and anti-Christian values so pervasively and convincingly portrayed in the media.

We dismiss it as "only entertainment," but there is plenty of research that proves that people become more violent when they are exposed to violence portrayed on the screen. I believe we also become less shocked by acts of cruelty and injustice. We find ourselves mimicking the styles of speech and dress modeled in the media. Dangerous and destructive sexual practices begin to seem normal.

For some the best answer may be to banish the television and not go to movies at all. I believe most of us, however, can find much of value in the media if we learn to exercise discretion. Specifically I recommend the following steps:

- Rationally choose what you are going to watch or read. Don't just flop down in front of the set or pick up any magazine or book that's handy. Use a television guide, such as Ted Baehr's *Movieguide*, to make intelligent choices;

- Think about and discuss what you see or read. Compare the values portrayed with biblical teaching. This is especially good to do with children;

- Be responsible about the amount of time you spend with media. The average American spends about four hours a day with television, another three and a half with radio, and about a half-hour with a newspaper. While radio may be used in the background while you are doing other things, television is usually foreground. I think it is irresponsible to habitually spend such a large percentage of one's discretionary time on something that accomplishes little if anything.

---

1. See Revelation 11:9-10
2. "The Global Village," Special section in the *Los Angeles Times*, 20 October 1992, 2.

CHAPTER EIGHT

Improve Your One-on-One Communication Skills

We found in the last chapter that face-to-face, one-on-one communication is the most powerful, although often the most costly, form of communication. Its effectiveness comes from the fact that as a speaker, you can use all sense channels. You can also make use of continuous feedback to adapt your message. Finally, social norms make it awkward for a person to ignore you in a one-on-one situation.

One-on-one communication is expensive. Both individuals must invest a lot of time — for traveling and sometimes for preparation. Because face-to-face communication has something of the feel of a social event, it may also take some time to get down to the point of the meeting, thus making the time investment even greater. We need to think about how we can best use this powerful but costly form of communication.

Clarifying Your Purpose

As I mentioned earlier in the book, one of the basic ways to communicate more effectively is to clearly understand your purpose. If your goal is unclear, you can't know when you have reached it. As someone once said, "He who aims at nothing will surely hit it."

To improve your communication be clear about your purpose.

Consider these purposes for one-on-one communication:

- pleasure,
- friendship,
- recruitment,
- information,
- meeting a need,
- evangelism.

You may be able to clarify and achieve your purpose better if you prepare an agenda. You can list the topics to be discussed, any decisions that need to be made, and an ending time. If it is a business meeting, you could give the agenda to the person with whom you are meeting. Even if you don't share it, having worked out an agenda in your mind will make your meeting more productive.

Prepare an agenda for a meeting even if you do not present it.

Listening

Listening is so important that I devoted an entire chapter to it earlier. One of the great advantages of one-on-one communication is the ease of communication both ways. Here are a few reminders on listening techniques.

- Probe for depth. People are often reluctant to reveal their deep thoughts for fear of rejection or disinterest. Probes are simple statements that encourage a person to say more. The simplest is to just say, "Uh huh?" with rising tone, as if asking a question, and then wait.

- Give your undivided attention. Don't be reading, looking around, or thinking about other things.

- Don't be too quick to come back with a similar situation in your own life because it may be quite different and interfere with your ability to understand the other person.

- Don't devalue the other person's trauma or joy. "Well if you think that's bad, let me tell you about the time. . . . " "My wife had one even better than that. . . . " We are to "Rejoice with those who rejoice; mourn with those who mourn,"[1] not try to outdo their stories.

- Don't "spiritualize" the other person's feelings away. "Sister, you shouldn't be under this burden. Just give it to Jesus and He will give you victory." Telling a person she shouldn't feel as she does only adds to her guilt and makes her less willing to express her feelings.

- Make feelings explicit. If the other person seems to be denying or not experiencing the emotions you would expect, you might gently help him express feelings by saying something like, "How do you feel about that?" or "That must feel terrible" or "I think that would make me really angry."

Setting Time Limits

To increase efficiency specify an ending time as well as a beginning time for meetings. My wife, Sylvia Nash, CEO of Christian Healthcare Network, sometimes uses what she calls "five minute stand-up meetings" with her staff. They meet in the hall, everyone stands, and they discuss a single topic. There is little temptation for the meeting to become prolonged.

If you have a business meeting with someone who tends to take too much time, have it at her office so you can leave when you want to. It's much easier to leave someone else's office than to kick someone out of yours!

Often a problem can be avoided by stating the time limit at the beginning of the meeting. On a phone call you could say, "I only have ten minutes right now. Will that be enough time, or shall we reschedule?"

You may also need to set limits as to when you can receive calls or callers. Once when I called on a pastor, I was told he was devoting the morning to study and asked not to be disturbed unless it was very important. I decided I could call at another time, and I respected his discipline!

Set time limits for meetings.

Even personal friendships need to have limits. Proverbs says it best, "Seldom set foot in your neighbor's house—too much of you, and he will hate you."[2] In my younger days I was sometimes insensitive about leaving some friends' house at a reasonable hour. I got the hint when the friend said to his wife, "Honey, I think we ought to go to bed. These people might want to go home!"

Setting Limits in Intimacy

At one time society had highly developed rules about "proper" contact between people. For example, women didn't speak to men unless they had been properly introduced. While many of the rules were silly, they did provide helpful standards for guarding against inappropriate intimacy. Today we are pretty much on our own in setting these limits. (I do recommend Jerry Jenkins' book, *Hedges: Loving Your Marriage Enough to Protect It,* which gives practical means of setting standards for contact with the opposite sex.)

Some degree of closeness is necessary if both parties are to have freedom to speak honestly and deeply. But too much privacy can easily lead to an unhealthy relationship that ends in sin. As I am writing this I am experiencing the pain of fresh wounds caused by a loved and trusted pastor friend who has fallen into sexual sin. Because he did not set wise boundaries, a wonderful ministry has been destroyed and thousands of people are suffering.

Set limits in intimacy.

In the absence of societal guidelines, we need to set up our own rules, and enforce them consistently.

- Don't be totally alone for significant periods of time with a member of the opposite sex. I've heard Billy Graham won't even ride in an elevator alone with a woman.

- Find a meeting place that provides some privacy but not too much. For example, my office door has a large window in it, so anyone passing in the hall can look in. Before the window was installed, I always kept the door open when I had students in my office.

- Be careful about bodily contact. A warm hug as a greeting seems natural for many people, but it should be short and not involve genital contact. Holding hands, touching feet or knees, and sitting too close together can all give a message that you would welcome sexual intimacy, regardless of the words you say.

■ Be careful where your eyes wander and how you dress. Men are tempted to sneak looks at women's breasts and thighs. Women are tempted to reveal these parts so men will look at them! Both parties are playing with fire.

■ Limit the amount of time you spend with a member of the opposite sex.

■ Don't depend on the other person to set limits. Men sometimes think it's the woman's responsibility to say no. Subordinates sometimes think their superior is the one to set limits. However, we are all individually responsible before God.

■ Include a third person. It is often wise to include a third person when talking to someone of the opposite sex. This should be a requirement if you are visiting the person at home, in a hotel room, or any other place where sexual sin would be easy. The third person could be your spouse, secretary, assistant, or associate.

■ Be accountable to someone. If you are placed in situations where compromise is possible, make yourself accountable to someone who will ask hard questions. Knowing you are going to have to defend your choices will help deter you. Another person may sense dangers you don't. If you find yourself strongly attracted to another person, confess this to a person to whom you are accountable. Do not confess your attraction to the object of your attraction!

■ Recognize the signs and be ready to back away if necessary. Don't assume that just because one or both of you are happily married, you will be unattracted to each other. If you find yourself thinking a lot about another person, idealizing him or her, or finding excuses to be together, recognize that you are in trouble and back away.

■ Avoid even the appearance of evil. It is not enough to be pure, you must also appear to be pure.[3]

Setting Limits Regarding Competence

In a relationship in which you are helping someone, you need to be aware of the limits to your competence. For example, I am very competent at advising students about what courses to take and about routine aspects of college life; however, if I have a student who is deeply emotionally disturbed, I am "out of my depth" and must refer the student to the university's counseling center. I believe it would be immoral of me to try to help someone whose problem is beyond my area of competence.

If you are in a helping relationship with others, you should think through the limits of your expertise and be prepared to refer a person who needs more help than you can provide. Just because a needy person has confidence that you can help does not mean you can, or that you are the best person to do so.

> **Ethical Point**
> Don't attempt to give help you are not competent to give. Refer the person to someone with appropriate counseling skills.

Getting Started

I grew up in a small town in Oregon where you said "Hi" to everyone you met on the street. I still find it easy to strike up conversations with perfect strangers. It sometimes embarrasses my wife.

How do you get a conversation started with strangers? S.I. Hawakawa gives a great illustration:

Let us suppose that we are on the roadside struggling with a flat tire. A not-very-bright-looking but friendly youth comes up and asks, "Got a flat tire?" If we insist on taking his words literally, we will regard this as an extremely silly question and our answer may be, "Can't you see I have, you dumb ox?" If we pay no attention to what the words say, however, and understand his meaning, we will return his gesture of friendly interest by showing equal friendliness, and in a short while he may help us to change the tire.[4]

Hawakawa goes on in a footnote to quote Dr. Karl Menninger commenting on this passage in terms of its psychological meaning:

Hello — I see you are in trouble. I'm a stranger to you but I might be your best friend now that I have a chance to be, if I had any assurance that my friendship would be welcomed. Are you approachable? Are you a decent fellow? Would you appreciate it if I helped you? I would like to do so but I don't want to be rebuffed. This is what my voice sounds like. What does your voice sound like?[5]

Dr. Menninger explains that the reason the youth does not simply say directly, "I would be glad to help you," is because, "people are too timid and mutually distrustful to be so direct. They want to hear one another's voices. People need assurance that others are just like themselves."

Often in the early phases of a relationship, the words are of little importance. It's non-verbal aspects like the tone of voice and facial expressions that do the work. As a college professor, I see this sort of thing fairly often. . . .

Pay attention to facial expression and tone of voice. They are often more important than the actual words spoken.

She: Hi. Uh. Did you understand what we are supposed to do for that . . . (assignment, paper, etc.)?

He: Well, I think (gives a couple of details).

She: Oh. That's kind of what I thought. You got yours done yet?

He: No, but I'm working on it.

Now, actually the words are almost totally meaningless because the real message is in the tone of voice, the face, and the body language. She is saying, "See how cute I am? Wouldn't you like to go out with me? I'm really friendly. You would like me."

So why doesn't she say this right out? Because it would hurt too much if the man turned her down. If he doesn't take the bait, she hasn't risked much (she was just asking about an assignment) so she doesn't hurt so much.

Because it's risky to start a new relationship, we have ritualized some relatively safe ways to get started. "Hi," ("Hello," "How do you do?" etc.) "Did it rain last night out your way?" or "How about them (supply name of local team)?"

Here are some additional ideas to help you start talking to people.

- Start with talk where easy agreement is possible. It could certainly be more creative than the weather or sports, but these will work.

- Remember that the nonverbal aspects of communication are important. Give a firm handshake, look the person directly in the eye, smile, give your full attention.

- You may be tempted to move too quickly to the "real" point of the meeting, perhaps to invite someone to a service or to sell a product. You will probably be more effective if you spend some time letting the other person get to know and trust you. We Americans are impatient to get down to business, but we forget that the basis for many business decisions is personal friendship and trust. The same is certainly true for evangelism.

■ I find it helpful to ask some questions about the other person. I'm always curious about what people do, where they grew up, their family, etc. As long as the questions are not overly personal, most people like to talk about themselves.

Ten Principles for Effective Interpersonal Communication

Now that you have started a conversation, how do you bring it to a successful conclusion? The following principles will help. The first five stem from the work of psychologists such as Maslow, Allport, Rogers, and others, the last five reflect the somewhat later thinking of Watzlawick, Beavin and Jackson, and others.[6]

1. Openness

Openness implies a willingness to disclose personal information, to react honestly to information given by the other person, and to "own" feelings and thoughts.

Scripture is remarkably open. If God had hired a public relations firm to write the Bible, we never would have known about David's adultery or Noah's drunkenness. But it is these great heroes of the faith who were far from perfect that encourage the rest of us sinners.

When I was going through a particularly difficult "passage" in my own life, I sought help from two different counselors. I think their difference illustrates the concept of openness. The first, a psychologist, said very little except to ask some pointed questions. He told me nothing about himself, and seemed to be cold, judgmental, and aloof. I dreaded my sessions with him. I felt lonely, vulnerable, and condemned. He may have helped me some, but it wasn't a pleasant experience.

134

Be honest about your feelings and even your failings.

On the other hand, my pastor reacted to my situation with great sympathy and even shared similarly trying situations from his own life. He was not ashamed to admit that he too was a sinner. I felt warm, safe, and cared for when I talked with him. I felt he heard me and understood. He helped me a great deal. He was open.

I don't mean to suggest here that pastors are always more sympathetic than psychologists. It could have easily been the other way around. Perhaps the psychologist believed I would profit more from direct confrontation. But I at least felt that I received more help from the warmer individual.

The idea of "owning" a thought or feeling is to admit it is yours. That is simple enough to say, harder to do. In my writing, including this book, I find I have to constantly go back and reword abstract principles so I express them as personal convictions and experiences.

People are not as interested in, for example, "Five Principles of Prayer," as they are in hearing about what has worked for you. In past years the "academically correct" way to write was as if the writer were not a real person. Now we know writing and speaking will be more powerful if they are personal.

2. Empathy

Empathy is the skill of understanding and experiencing the feelings of another person. It is not the same as sympathy, which is to care about how another person is feeling. A person with empathy will actually experience some of the pain or joy felt by a friend. That's empathy!

135

Develop the skill of empathy.
Practice thinking how another person is feeling.

Developing empathy is a little like learning to act! A great actor will be able to actually *experience* the emotions he is portraying. I remember one particular actor with whom I worked. He could give a very convincing portrayal of any emotion I asked for, and he could do it quickly! How did he do it? He thought about a time in his own life when he had experienced that particular emotion, then just let himself experience the feeling again. His acting was natural because his emotions were real.

To know what another person is feeling, we must first learn to experience and understand our own emotions. During my early years my father modeled the good English virtue of a "stiff upper lip," so it wasn't until my 30s that I learned it was not only OK, but actually very healthy to experience and express emotions. As I became more able to experience my own feelings, I found I could also more easily feel what others were experiencing.

Sometimes the other person doesn't seem to be feeling what you might expect in the situation. If a man's wife has just deserted him, he may say he's doing OK, but you can be pretty sure he's not! When someone is in that situation, you can register some of the pain you feel (empathy) and say something like, "Oh! You must really be hurting."

At times strong feelings will leak into the tone of voice and give away an emotion the person is denying. You can tactfully point out, "Your voice sounds really angry!" This may help the person to "come clean" about her feelings. Sometimes people show in their face what their words seem to deny. You can give some feedback, "How are you feeling? You really look sad."

3. Supportiveness

The term as used here has two components: (1) to describe rather than judge, and (2) to be tentative rather than certain in our judgment.

In the chapter on listening skills, I mentioned that premature judging will interfere with our understanding of the speaker's message. We need to make sure we really understand the message before we begin to evaluate it. This same technique is an important part of being supportive. When people know they are truly being heard rather than judged, they feel less threatened.

Try to hear and understand rather than judge another.

When making descriptive statements, you can describe the situation objectively and also your reaction. You could say, for example, "It makes me feel so sad to hear that you and Betty are splitting up." Sadness is not a judgment (that is, a statement about right and wrong), just an emotional reaction. Often we are too quick to judge and too slow to really understand the situation. Scripture says we should be quick to listen and slow to speak.[7]

Our communication will be more honest, open, and effective if we learn to say the two little words, *"to me."* Sometimes we are guilty of confusing how the world actually is with how we see it. By saying, "It seems to me," I am acknowledging that what I am putting forth is my *perception* or opinion, not necessarily objective truth. I am making the confession that I am fallible. We all need to realize our judgments are not the same thing as objective facts. Proverbs says, "The first to present his case seems right, till another comes forward and questions him."[8]

Learn to say, "to me."

When we turn to revealed truth, God's Word, we have the right to be more dogmatic, but even here we must be careful because our understanding or interpretation of Scripture is not necessarily the correct one.[9]

We can't even be too sure about things we have seen with our own eyes. Communication professors have sometimes illustrated the unreliability of eyewitness reports by staging a fake hold-up during class. An armed robber bursts into the classroom, robs the professor, then leaves. The professor asks the students to quickly write down what they saw because they were all witnesses to the crime. The students don't know at this point that the crime was staged.

Later, the professor has the students read what they have written, and many discrepancies arise. The professor eventually confesses the ruse, and invites the "robber" back into the classroom so the students can take a good look at him and see where they went wrong in their descriptions.

By qualifying our statements and even our eyewitness accounts, we seem less extreme and more humble. Besides, when we acknowledge that we might be wrong, we are more likely to be open to other ideas, and in the end we may learn something!

Having said all this, we need to realize that for Christians there is a time for confrontation and correction. Paul wrote, "If someone is caught in a sin, you who are spiritual should restore him gently. But watch yourselves, or you also may be tempted."[10] This verse tells us a lot about confrontation. First, it is to be done by those "who are spiritual." I would take this to mean those who are seeking to walk closely in obedience to God and who are not harboring sin in their own lives.[11] Next, the purpose is restoration, rather than punishment. Third, we are to be gentle. It's easier to be gentle when we recognize the truth of the next admonition: "watch yourselves, or you also may be tempted." We are made of the same fallible stuff that the fallen one is!

A young Christian woman announced to my wife and me that she was planning to move in with her boyfriend. When she sensed our displeasure with this arrangement, she said, "I thought you would be more supportive of me." My wife answered wisely, "We want you to know that we love you dearly, and we always will regardless of what you do. But there is no way we can support what you are doing because it is wrong. It goes against Scripture and everything we believe."

While we do need to take a definite moral stand, we should always remember that we are not infallible and that we should treat others with love and respect.

4. Positiveness

There are two ways we can express positiveness: (1) through positive attitudes and (2) through acknowledging the importance of the other person.

Very often the same basic idea will be more effective when expressed in positive terms rather than negative. Consider the following:

Negative: (To the song leader): I hate the rock music you are using in the services.
Positive: I really love it when we sing the old hymns.

Negative: That dress makes you look fat.
Positive: I think you look best in the black dress.

Express your thoughts in positive terms rather than negative.

Expressing positive attitudes about people is even more important. Many people do not feel cared for or valued. Some of those you care about deeply may not even know that you do. Proverbs says, "Better is open rebuke than hidden love."[12]

Unfortunately, our hunger to be loved and appreciated is so great that we are susceptible to flatterers. To flatter is to say something complimentary about a person when it is not sincere, for the purpose of getting some advantage. Flattery is sinful and destructive.[13] But a sincere expression of appreciation or friendship or love will greatly facilitate communication.

5. Equality

Every person is made in God's image, loved of God, and consequently of great value. Scripture says God does not show partiality[14]; therefore, I conclude that differences in status based on factors such as gender, race, education, occupation, wealth, physical appearance, age, etc., are products of our sinfulness.

In order for society to work, some people must be in authority over others, and we are told to obey the authorities[15] unless they command us to do something directly against God's teaching.[16] So, some differences in position or function are necessary, but these should not be interpreted as differences in the worth of human beings.

Paul points out that in the body of Christ (the church) all parts are equally important, though some may be more prominent than others.[17] Even in the church we are surrounded by artificial differences in status caused by sin. Justice requires us to fight against these. The Scripture is full of condemnations against injustice.[18]

Recognize that we are all equal in the eyes of God. Fight against injustice.

How can we keep inequality from affecting our communication?

- We must avoid racial and gender slurs. (This may be more difficult than it at first seems because status differences of race and gender are so much a part of our culture.)

- Bosses should speak to subordinates with the respect suitable for an equal. Inequality pops up when bosses assume their higher position makes them more valuable as people.

- We should be careful not to interrupt another person, implying that what we have to say is more important.

- Avoid correcting another person's message. My wife is a more vivid storyteller than I am, but I sometimes pay more attention to detail; therefore, I am frequently tempted to correct her stories. That proves to be counterproductive because it puts her down in front of the listeners. Any minor inaccuracies that go uncorrected rarely affect the outcome anyway.

- Avoid "should" and "ought" statements. These statements imply an unequal relationship.

Unfortunately, the temptation to appear superior by putting another person down is always with us. I think if we fully appreciated all we are and have in Christ, that "need" would go away!

6. Confidence

A person who shows confidence will be more effective in interpersonal communication. Here are some things you can do to convey confidence in interpersonal situations.

- Introduce yourself;

- Introduce a topic of conversation without waiting for others to start it;

- Ask questions of other people, involving them in the conversation;

- Ask others about themselves: What do you think? Do you agree?

If you feel you can't do these things because you are too timid or uneducated consider the Apostle Paul. Even though he had the highest education available, and certainly had an impressive pedigree, he came to feel that it was of no value. His confidence came from knowing Christ.[19]

Develop confidence based on your value as a child of God. Know the difference between confidence and cockiness.

Confidence grows through experience, but we have to be willing to take some risks. In college I was quite lacking in confidence. The Lord convicted me about it, so I made a pact with Him that for a time I would do anything ministry-oriented that I was asked to do. Well, that week someone asked me to preach at a street meeting! I had never done anything like that before, but with the Lord's help I did a good job and my confidence grew.

7. Immediacy

So often in communication situations we are distracted with other pressures and thoughts. While talking on the phone, I may also be reading, watching TV, or even typing! My phone conversation gets only part of my attention. To be effective in interpersonal communication, we need to give our full attention to the person with whom we are talking. Consider these actions:

- maintain good eye contact without looking around at others;

- sit erect, even lean forward;

- sit close to the other person;

- smile;

- use the person's name;

- make sure the other person knows she is being heard and understood. Ask questions or give feedback as necessary;

- compliment the other person: "I appreciate your comments on this."

Give your full attention to the person with whom you are communicating.

I admit this is one of my weaknesses. When students come to see me, I have to make a real effort to "be there." As I mentioned earlier, it helps if I move away from my desk, computer, and phone to another part of my office where I have a small, round table. I imagine it must be very disconcerting to a student who finally works up his courage to talk to the prof, only to find the prof is not really all there!

8. Interaction Management

Interpersonal communication will be more effective if both parties talk. At times the situation breaks down because one party is either reluctant to talk, or else dominates. A skilled communicator can help regulate the flow. Here's how.

- Don't dominate. If you are talking too much, ask a question.

- Don't be afraid of a little silence. You may find yourself talking too much because the other person seems reluctant to talk. Some people are slow starters, but given enough time and encouragement they will talk.

- If a person is reluctant to talk, reward her by saying "uh huh," at appropriate places, smiling, and nodding. Ask follow-up questions if necessary.

- If a person talks too much, you could break in by saying something like, "Can I respond to that?"

- If a person tends to cut you off prematurely, look away from him at moments he would cut you off. You can also indicate, "wait" by holding up your hand, palm toward him, when he starts to interrupt. You can also say something like, "Let me just finish this."

Develop skills in drawing the other person out and also getting the person to hear you fully.

9. Other-Orientation

It is natural for us to be self-centered, but our communication will be more effective if we are other-centered. The skill of empathy, discussed earlier, is helpful, but more than skill is required. I can only be other-oriented if I am humble enough to see that others are as important as I am. Strangely, humility can come from understanding how important I actually am!

Realize how important you are so you can afford to value other people!

Let me explain. If I feel inadequate and unloved, I bring to every interaction such a strong awareness of my own need that I won't be able to be concerned about others' needs. If, on the other hand, I feel adequate and loved, I won't try to "get" something from every conversation. Having no exaggerated sense of my own needs, I am free to pay attention to the needs of others.

How does one feel adequate and loved? To feel "important" you may seek academic degrees and honors, achievement, possessions, etc., but the best way is to believe what God says. I could cite hundreds of verses, but probably the familiar John 3:16 passage says it best: "God so loved the world that He gave His one and only Son that whoever believes in Him shall not perish but have eternal life." If the Almighty God loves you that much, you are pretty important!

If your experience is like mine, there is some discrepancy between what you know from the Bible and what you feel. I believe our relationship with God is in many respects like our relationship with a person. That is, our confidence in Him grows gradually over time and with experience and intimacy. So, the best way to feel how important you are to God is to spend enough time with Him so that you deeply believe and trust Him.

God sometimes nudges the process along by allowing crises into our lives. I remember walking on a deserted beach one winter day several years ago thinking about my sorry situation: my marriage was in trouble, I had financial difficulties, a close friend had just fallen into sexual sin, I was under incredible pressure at work, and my brother was dying of cancer.

As I turned in my desperation to the Lord, I felt such a sense of overwhelming love and peace I shall never forget it. He did not make all the troubles go away, but that wasn't so important. I knew and *felt*, more than I ever had before, His presence with me and His love for me. In that confidence I knew I could face whatever problems lay ahead.

I once heard evangelist Leighton Ford say after the death of his son, "I have felt the bottom, and it is firm."

In my case, counseling and some friends in a small Bible study group also aided my growth in feeling OK about myself. I discovered that I had a hard time feeling good about myself because as a child I felt I could never please my father. I also confused my feelings about my Heavenly Father with those of my earthly father. Getting some of those things straightened out in my mind helped.

We sometimes get into trouble when we compare ourselves with others. I remember a "pity party" I had when a coworker received a promotion I thought I should have had. I'm afraid I had a hard time "rejoicing with those who rejoice," on that day. Why? Because I wanted to feel good about myself *in comparison to* someone else. What a terrible and destructive thing it is if I can only feel good when someone else feels bad.

If I really understand how much God values me, I won't have to compare myself to others. Even though He has made others more talented, richer, more handsome, and taller, He could not possibly love them any more than He loves me! When I feel secure in God's love (I still don't always), I have a wonderful freedom to express His love to others. Because it is limitless, I don't diminish my own supply by giving it away! If I know I am loved of God, it doesn't matter so much if humans love me or not, so I'm free to take some chances.

Does God want us to be "other-oriented"? Clearly he does.[20] Perhaps the most spectacular evidence of this is in the famous "love chapter," 1 Corinthians 13. In the midst of a discussion of the mechanics of service (our gifts), Paul breaks into a sublime chapter on the *motivation* for service (love).

How does the idea of "other orientation" work out in practical ways? Jesus gave us the basic principle in what has come to be called the Golden Rule: "Do to others what you would have them do to you."[21]

In any situation you need to think of what you would want if you were the other person, then act accordingly. This won't work perfectly because we are not able to entirely understand the situation of the other person, but it is a very good place to start. Along that line, here are some practical ideas.

- Let the other person know you appreciate and value him.

- Ask the other person's views and opinions.

- Take the time to understand the other person. Ask for clarification if necessary.

- Be honest, but if honesty would hurt the other person, do so with tact and sensitivity.

- Give feedback. Agree when appropriate.

- Value the other person's feelings. Allow or even invite her to express emotions. You could ask, "How do you feel about that?"

10. Role-shifting

Another way you can improve your interpersonal communication effectiveness is to notice the predominant communication style of the other person and adjust your style accordingly.

Adopt a communication style similar to that of the person with whom you are communicating.

People express themselves with many different styles. Researchers have developed almost as many different category schemes for describing these styles. None are perfect, but some are quite helpful. I like this one, derived from Jungian psychology.[22] There are four distinct styles. Any given communicator will likely use some of each, but one style will tend to predominate.

1. Intuiting. This person is imaginative, creative, innovative. He may also be impersonal and challenging. He asks, "why?" and often has good ideas. He can go off on a tangent.

2. Thinking. The thinker analyzes, orders, weighs options, reflects rationally, and gathers facts. She is systematic and information-centered.

3. Feeling. The feeler is warm, friendly, and supportive. He injects humor and personal anecdotes into his conversations. He talks a lot, is animated, and has empathy.

4. Sensing. This person reacts quickly to what she senses, is competitive, goes for results, and lives in the here-and-now. She can be abrupt, impatient, and controlling.

Your interpersonal communication will be more effective to the extent that you can adjust your style to match the style of the other person. For example:

- If the person is an intuitor, expect him to look for alternate ways to solve the problem, but also realize the intuitor may take you off on a tangent. Be prepared to bring the conversation back;

- If the person is a thinker, give her plenty of facts and figures to analyze;

- If the person is a feeler, deal with the emotional aspects of the issue;

- If the person is a senser, anticipate that she will understand the situation quickly and want to move to action.

Chapter Summary

Interpersonal communication is powerful and expensive, so you must be careful to use it effectively. Start with being clear about your purpose. Next, practice effective listening techniques. Also think through limits in time and intimacy.

Some communication is ritualized yet plays an important role in getting past the awkward beginning. "How do you do?" should not be interpreted as an honest request for details on how you are doing, but rather as a polite ritual. Nonverbal factors such as a firm handshake and eye contact help to establish and continue a relationship.

The chapter concludes with a discussion of 10 principles for effective communication: openness, empathy, supportiveness, positiveness, equality, confidence, immediacy, interaction management, other-orientation, and role-shifting.

1. See Romans 12:15.

2. See Proverbs 25:17.

3. See 2 Corinthians 8:20-21.

4. S.I. Hawakawa, *Language in Thought and Action*, 2nd ed. (New York: Harcourt, Brace & World, 1964, 78.

5. Dr. Karl Menninger, *Love against Hate*, 1942.

6. The particular formulation of these ten principles is adapted from Joseph A. DeVito, *The Interpersonal Communication Book*, 6th ed. (New York: Harper Collins, 1992), a highly readable and practical college text on the subject.

7. See James 1:19.

8. See Proverbs 18:17.

9. See 2 Peter 1:20.

10. See Galatians 6:1

11. See, for example, Matthew 7:3-5.

12. See Proverbs 27:5.

13. See, for example: Proverbs 26:28; 29:5; Romans 16:18; Jude 16.

14. See Galatians 3:28; Acts 10:34-35; James 2:1-9.

15. See Romans 13:1-7; Titus 3:1-2; 1 Peter 2:13-15.

16. See Acts 5:29.

17. See 1 Corinthians 12:12-31.

18. See, for example: Exodus 23:6; Amos 5:6-7.

19. See Philippians 3:2-9.

20. See, for example, Galatians 6:2; Philippians 2:4.

21. See Matthew 7:12.

22. Adapted from Mark Knapp and Anita Vangelisti, *Interpersonal Communication and Human Relationships*, 2nd ed. (Heedham Heights, Mass: Allyn and Bacon, 1992), 365.

CHAPTER NINE

Use the Best of Both Mass and Interpersonal Communication

itler's effective use of radio and film and the early
success of Communist propaganda led to the fear during the 1930s and 1940s that the mass media were
almost irresistible. So when Paul Lazarsfeld[1] and others of Columbia University did some research on media effects during
the election campaign of 1940, their results could hardly have
been a greater surprise. They were trying to find out if radio or
newspapers would be more influential in changing the mind of
voters. They found that few voters changed their mind, and
those who did were influenced primarily by other people they
knew, not the mass media.

The Influence of Opinion Leaders

Fortunately for us they dug a little deeper and made some
observations that have fundamentally changed the way we use
mass media today. They found certain people are unusually influential in the lives of others. (They called these "opinion leaders.") They also discovered that opinion leaders use mass media

to keep up-to-date in their areas of leadership.

The greatest power of the mass media to influence is indirect, filtered through one or more layers of opinion leaders. Lazarsfeld called this phenomenon the "two-step flow" of influence from the mass media. It might better be called a "multi-step flow" because we now know that opinion leaders themselves also have opinion leaders who use mass media to keep informed.

It's helpful here to make a distinction between knowing something and deciding to take action. These days we find out about most things directly from the media but often don't decide to act until another person we know has persuaded us to do so. So, knowledge usually comes directly from the media, but influence to act comes indirectly through other people, opinion leaders.

Communicate through opinion leaders.

Who are these opinion leaders? Katz and Lazarsfeld[2] went on to study the characteristics of these leaders and found them to be surprisingly like those they influence. We are not so much influenced by "world class" experts as we are by people very much like us who are just a bit more knowledgeable on a particular topic than we are. These are family members or people with whom we work or socialize. They are people with similar value systems. Opinion leaders are aware that people seek their opinion. They want to maintain their expertise so they can look good when people ask their advice.

Opinion leaders are usually of the same social status and frequently of the same age category as their followers. In some topics age makes a difference.

Opinion leadership is specialized. The woman who is influential in grocery shopping is probably not influential in fashion. It is unusual for a person to be an opinion leader in several fields.

151

Opinion leaders are not just sources of information. Because of their close relationship with their followers, they can apply social pressure to conform and provide social support when their followers follow their advice.[3] While the media can deliver information well, the unique power of the opinion leader lies in an ability to influence by social pressure and support.

An opinion leader is more interested in the topic than her followers are, but the followers must have some degree of interest, or they will not seek information. Without followers there is no leader!

An obvious strategy for influencing people through the mass media is to reach opinion leaders so they will influence their followers. How does one do this?

- Opinion leaders have a higher interest in the subject than most people, so they are more likely to seek out information. If you put the information where they can easily find it, they will!

- If you find out what kind of people are opinion leaders in a particular area, you can design media to reach them more effectively. For example, the "soap operas" are called that because soap manufacturers realized that women with families who are at home during the daytime buy a great deal of soap and influence others in their choices. They created dramas designed very carefully to appeal to these women.

- Opinion leaders are more likely to use specialized media, specific to the area of their leadership. If you wanted to reach those who influence car purchases, for example, you might advertise in such publications as *Car and Driver.*

- If people are not interested in the topic you wish to influence them in, there will be no opinion leaders. But you can use the media to provide a background of information and build interest.

The Decision-making Process

How do people make choices? Paul outlines the steps in Romans 10:13-14: "Everyone who calls on the name of the Lord will be saved. How, then, can they call on the One they have not believed in? And how can they believe in the One of whom they have not heard? And how can they hear without someone preaching to them?"

By listing the steps in reverse order, Paul establishes that each step depends on the previous one. He lists three steps.

1. Hearing (receiving information),
2. Believing (processing the information to come to a conclusion),
3. Calling (acting on the information).

Paul's three steps correspond well to a four-step model from researcher Everett Rogers.[4]

1. Knowledge
2. Persuasion
3. Decision
4. Confirmation

You will notice that the first three steps are essentially the same as Paul's, followed by a fourth step, confirmation.

These simple steps are often over-looked, to our peril. Paul is telling us not to start the process by trying to force a decision (they can't decide unless they believe) or by persuasion to believe (they can't believe without information). We must start by providing information. Responsible decisions require accurate information.

Ethical Point
It is immoral to try to push people into decisions until they have the necessary information.

Too often Christians have concentrated their efforts at the

153

decision step. In today's world we can no longer assume people have enough *information* to make a good choice. I believe it is immoral to bully, trick, cajole, or otherwise influence people to make a decision before they have enough information to do so freely. Ethical persuasion (including evangelism), therefore, must begin with information!

Present information before urging people to make a choice.

Rogers adds another insight: "Mass media channels are relatively more important at the knowledge function, and interpersonal channels are relatively more important at the persuasion function in the innovation-decision process.[5] This suggests some additional strategies if you want to influence people to make a decision.

- If your audience lacks *information*, this can probably be provided most rapidly and economically through the media. This could take many forms, including radio, television, videotapes, books, pamphlets, newsletters, etc. For example, Church on the Way, pastored by Jack Hayford, gives visitors a free videotape telling about the church. Saddleback Community Church, pastored by Rick Warren, makes extensive use of newspaper advertising to provide information about the church. Willow Creek Community Church, pastored by Bill Hybels, uses the strategy of "seeker services," designed for people at the information-seeking level.

- Church members could be provided with printed brochures and/or videotapes to use in introducing their friends to the church.

- Once audience members have some information, they need to be in contact with opinion leaders to influence them to act in appropriate ways. This strategy has long been used to good advantage by churches through such groups as Sunday School classes, training unions, women's groups, men's groups, youth groups, singles ministries, Circles of Concern, and many other such groups. These groups (or sub-groups) must be small enough so people can get to know each other individually.

Because opinion leaders have been found to be similar to their followers, small group leaders must either be similar to their group members or if they are not (for example, an adult teacher of junior high students), they should emphasize their similarity in important areas and seek to develop opinion leaders among group members.

Using Homophily

Everett Rogers reports that one of the factors associated with influence is what he calls "homophily," that is, similarity between leaders and followers. I remember experiences as a high school student in a tiny Baptist church in Oregon which illustrate this point. Sunday School classes were a crashing bore, taught by an older man who had taken on the task out of duty. He had little knowledge of high schoolers and less empathy for them. He seemed to interpret his task as getting through the printed lesson in the "quarterly." He lectured in a drone. There were few questions and no discussion. We dreaded it, though we knew the teacher was a good man doing the best he knew how.

In contrast, the young people's meeting in the evening was entirely lead by high schoolers. (There was a "sponsor," an older man who had the good sense to sit in the back and become invisible.) One of the group members planned the lesson and assigned "parts" to the others. Various high schoolers led singing, played piano, gave announcements, prayed, etc.

The presentations were often halting and disjointed and there were occasional fits of laughter, but we also had lively discussion of issues highly relevant to our lives. As a new Christian coming into this group, I was incredibly impressed with the passion and depth of commitment of these kids. They influenced me far more than any sermon I ever heard, and certainly much more than the Sunday School teacher. Why? Because their faith was real, and *because they were like me.*

Use communicators who are similar to their audience. If the communicator is different, he/she should emphasize similarities.

The principle of homophily (similarity) suggests some strategies.

- The people leading small groups should be as similar as possible in most ways to their followers (socially, economically, educationally), but they should be somewhat more knowledgeable and committed in spiritual matters.

- Group leaders who are different from their group (in age or education, for example) should emphasize similarities. It helps if they are honest about their own struggles. When I was a missionary, most people I met assumed I must be made of fundamentally different stuff than they were. That made it hard to minister because people didn't believe I had the same struggles they did.

Leading Group Discussions

If you are a group leader who might be seen by group members as being different (perhaps even because of Bible knowledge or level of commitment), you can structure group activities so that other group members have the chance to emerge as opinion leaders. If several members of the group are contributing to and supporting the ideas you are presenting, these ideas will be seen as a group norm and thus be more persuasive.

- Group activities should include plenty of opportunity for members to interact informally. As group leader you may see your main purpose as getting through a "lesson," but if your time together becomes a lecture, the group is not being used to best advantage. Remember, information can be more effectively provided by media or large group meetings. It is much more beneficial to group members to hear each other reflect Christian values, especially when members may perceive the teacher as being too different to be an opinion leader.

- Small groups should concentrate on helping people get to know each other so they can influence each other. Social activities can serve a serious spiritual purpose!

Encourage group interaction so members of the group can influence each other.

It is, of course, not enough that group members interact with each other. For them to influence each other spiritually, they need to interact at least some of the time about spiritual things. As a leader your main function is to set the agenda and keep the discussion more or less on track. Consider the following ideas.

- Set the agenda. People generally want to know what a meeting is about, so you have a great opportunity to steer the discussion by your initial statements. I try to choose a topic that is of relevance to the group, and to help members understand why it is important. By asking some initial questions, and/or presenting a bit of framework, I help people want to discuss the issue. I have found handing out copies of an agenda that lists the topic, several questions, and Scripture references works well.

- Ask questions. I like application questions because they start people thinking about how they can *use* the information. You can ask how a passage or principle from Scripture would apply in a particular situation.

- Wait for answers. If you are not used to leading a discussion format, you may have a tendency to ask a question, then if someone doesn't immediately answer it, you answer it yourself. That defeats your purpose of stimulating discussion. So just don't answer it. Wait a whole minute or more if necessary. It will seem like an eternity the first time you try it! Rephrase the question if necessary. Eventually, someone will venture an answer, then someone else, and a discussion will begin.

- Reward all responses. A wrong or inadequate answer takes as much courage to voice as a right answer. You want to make it safe to fail, or many members of the group won't participate. Try to find ways to reward wrong answers by saying things like, "That brings up an important issue." Or, "A lot of people feel that way." Or simply say, "OK. What do some of the rest of you think?"

- Seat people in a circle or at least a semicircle so they can see each other.

- Sit down with your group if the group size will allow. You will put yourself on the same level — symbolically as well as literally.

- Encourage others in the group to answer questions or comment, even on difficult or controversial points. Remember that the group will be more influenced by hearing the observations of its own members than in hearing yours. You could say, "What do you think about that, George?"

■ When the discussion drifts off the topic, you need some discernment. Perhaps the area it drifted into is even better than the original topic. When you have animated discussion of an important, spiritually relevant subject, it's probably better to let it go than to cut it off just for the sake of covering the points you had intended to cover.

For example, one week my "Sound Workshop" class got into a wonderful discussion of what it means to be a Christian working in secular broadcasting. It was energetic, almost everyone took part, and it contained deep spiritual content. The only problem was that I felt a little frustrated because it was not what I intended to cover that day. Sometimes the Spirit has a different agenda than we do!

However, when the discussion drifts away from spiritually profitable material, you can nudge it back on course by asking a question relevant to the main topic. If you allow one or a few members to regularly take the group on tangents, most members will feel frustrated.

■ Don't be overly ambitious about what you cover. Discussion takes time. Realize that what you lose in the number of topics you include, you more than make up for in impact. If you don't get to all the points on the agenda, some of the members will feel cheated. Just before time runs out you may be able to give some sense of completeness by briefly summarizing points you weren't able to cover earlier. You might also continue the topic at your next meeting.

Developing Media Forums

The name is dull, but this is a hot idea! A media forum combines the strength of mass media with the strength of interpersonal communication. It works like this. A group of people get together, listen to or view a media program, or read the same printed material, then discuss it as a group.[6]

Use media forums as an effective way to communicate information and move people to action.

The strength of media forums is that the information can be delivered effectively by a mass medium. The medium also sets the agenda for the discussion which follows. The discussion follows immediately, while people still have the facts in mind, and a great deal of interpersonal persuasion can take place. If the group is a decision-making body, a decision can be made right after the discussion.

Research done in rural India with a group listening to radio followed by structured discussion demonstrated that there was much more change in the media forum situation compared to listening to the radio alone.[7]

If it works, why isn't it used more widely? (1) a lot of people don't know about it, and (2) to make it work, listening groups must be organized. It's vastly easier just to send out media messages than it is to organize your listeners into discussion groups. To do that on a national scale would require an army of local agents, and a huge budget.

But, where groups already exist, it's a natural. Here are some ways you can use media forums to good advantage.

■ For Sunday School classes.
   Use a media presentation such as an audio- or video-tape for about 20 minutes, followed by 20 to 40 minutes of discussion. This combination will hold attention and get more results than the all-too-common novice Sunday School teacher will. And it's much easier and more fun for the teacher, who now becomes a discussion facilitator.

- For adult Bible study and prayer groups.

  Do you have a shortage of excellent teachers? Put 20 minutes or so of quality teaching on a videotape or even a live teacher in an auditorium, then break into small discussion and prayer groups.

- For Sunday services.

  Make them more effective by breaking the congregation into small groups for 20 minutes or so after the sermon (which would need to be compact). Pass out three or four discussion questions in printed form.

Here are some specific ideas for executing effective media forums.

- The "media" portion should be concise and require no more than half the total meeting time. It should be presented in a format that will invite discussion.

- The discussion group members should know before they watch the media presentation that they are going to discuss it. This will motivate them to pay more attention.

- The discussion leader should be given some instruction in advance about how to conduct the discussion. She should view herself as a facilitator, not an expert or teacher.

- The discussion leader should be given specific questions to discuss. These can be given to the group on handouts, an overhead, a blackboard, etc. Having specific questions will help keep the group on track.

- If there is some detailed information that would help members in discussion, perhaps this can be presented to the group on handouts, or to the discussion leader in a manual.

- If appropriate, the group should be challenged to make a decision either as a group (if group action would be appropriate) or as individuals. In other words, the "so what" question should be addressed.

161

Chapter Summary

Mass media are effective for communicating information, but people are more persuaded to take action by interpersonal interaction so most people turn to opinion leaders before making a decision. These leaders are people similar to themselves who are a bit more knowledgeable in a particular field. Opinion leaders can be reached by specialized media, and they in turn will spread their ideas among their followers. This idea is called the two-step flow of influence from the media.

An effective way to use the strengths of both mass media and interpersonal communication is through media forums. For example, a Sunday School class could watch a videotape for 20 minutes, then spend another 40 minutes in a structured discussion led by one group member.

1. Paul F. Lazarsfeld, Bernard Berelson, and Gaudent, *The People's Choice*, 3rd ed. (New York: Columbia University Press, 1968), 150ff.

2. Elihu Katz and Paul F. Lazarsfeld, *Personal Influence: The Part Played by People in the Flow of Mass Communication* (New York: Free Press, 1955), 31ff.

3. See Elihu Katz, "The Two-Step Flow of Communication," *Public Opinion Quarterly* (Spring, 1957).

4. Everett M. Rogers and F. Floyd Shoemaker, *Communication of Innovations*, 2nd ed. (New York: Free Press, 1971), 103.

5. Ibid., 255.

6. For an excellent though brief discussion of media forums see Everett Rogers, and F. Floyd Shoemaker, *Communication of Innovations*, 2nd ed. (New York: Free Press, 1971), 261–63.

7. Paul Neurath, *Radio Farm Forum in India* (New Delhi: Government of India Press, 1960).

CHAPTER TEN

Understand How New
Ideas Spread

A nother very helpful line of research comes from anthropology and rural sociology. This research deals with how new ideas spread across a culture or from group to group. The process is called, "diffusion of innovations." Everett Rogers,[1] whom I have mentioned in the previous chapter, has organized and summarized much of this very helpful data.

Dr. Rogers started off his career as an agricultural extension agent and became frustrated because it was so difficult to get farmers to adopt new techniques which could greatly improve their yields. This frustration led him to a study of rural sociology and in particular the analysis of diffusion of innovations.

One of the things Dr. Rogers and others observed is that regardless

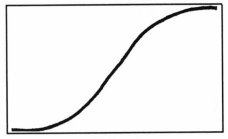

Figure 2
When new ideas are accepted,
they follow an "S" curve, like this.

of what the new idea is, people adopt it in a typical pattern. If you plot the number of people who have adopted the idea against time, you see that at first the curve rises very gradually because few people know about it or have the courage to try it. After a while people observe the success of those who have adopted the idea, and they try it themselves. As more people adopt it, the curve becomes steeper. When most of the people have adopted the new idea, the curve flattens out again while the last few laggards adopt. The curve has a kind of "S" shape. This pattern is always found, even though some ideas are adopted much more rapidly than others.

Differences in People According to When They Adopt Ideas

Rogers also found the people who were the first to adopt an idea were quite different than those who adopted later. He came up with the following categories.[2]

Innovators (The first 2.5 percent to adopt.)

These people love new ideas, and so are oriented to people, places, and publications on the cutting edge. Innovators have both the inclination and the resources to take risks. Some of their ideas fail, but they brush failure aside and go on.

This group is not very influential in the local community because they are too far ahead of the majority. They may be seen as weird. They don't socialize locally because they are oriented to new ideas, which tend to come from distant locations.

Early Adopters (The next 13.5 percent to adopt.)

These people are seen as respectable. They are often opinion leaders, more oriented to those around them, but still ahead of the majority. They are generally successful financially because of their willingness to try new ideas. Others seek their advice before trying a new idea.

Cultivate early adopters. They influence others.

Early Majority (The next 34 percent.)

These people are deliberate. "Be not the first by which the new is tried, nor the last to lay the old aside," would apply to them. They serve as opinion leaders for those who adopt later.

Late Majority (The next 34 percent.)

These people are skeptical. They are oriented to the tried and true and don't adopt a new idea until several around them have. Peer pressure helps them decide.

Laggards (The last 16 percent.)

They are traditional. They are oriented to the local situation, skeptical of anything from a distance. They are sometimes isolated socially, and they trust the past and distrust the new. They interact mostly with those who also hold their traditional views. They may eventually adopt a new idea because they can no longer function by the old method. They often adopt an idea too late, after the majority has adopted an even newer innovation. As a result, they are often poor and getting poorer.

In general, those who adopt ideas earlier are more educated, more literate, higher in social status, more wealthy, more likely to borrow money, and have more specialized skills. Those who adopt ideas earlier have greater empathy, are less dogmatic, better thinkers, more intelligent, more willing to take risks, more motivated, have higher aspirations, and are less fatalistic than those who adopt ideas later.

Not surprisingly, early adopters are more exposed to the media and are more likely to seek information about new ideas. They learn about new ideas sooner. Once they hear about them, they act more rapidly than the later adopters.

If you want to spread a new idea through a group, here are some helpful strategies.

- Concentrate your efforts on the early adopters, not the first few innovators. In other words, look for people who are innovative, but are also highly respected by the majority. If you are an outsider to the group, the innovators may be more willing to hear you, but they won't influence the larger group very much.

- Efforts to influence laggards or the late majority will be less productive because they are much less likely to trust new ideas or outsiders and because they are not role models for others.

- The greatest effort is best expended relatively early in the adoption process. The same amount of effort will have greater results if it influences those who become early adopters because they will influence others.

Characteristics of Innovations

Not all new ideas are equally easy to communicate. Rogers points out that the quality of an idea has a great deal to do with whether it will be adopted at all, and if so, how quickly. If you are trying to convince someone to adopt a new idea, try looking at the following aspects of the idea through that person's eyes.

Relative Advantage

Compared to other choices the person has, what is the cost-to-benefits ratio of the idea you are presenting? The higher the benefits and the lower the cost, the greater probability the idea will be adopted. Cost, as used here, does not refer only to money, but also to time, effort, and social status (appearing to be different.) Here are some ways you can emphasize the relative advantage of following Jesus.

- Emphasize the great value. Most parents want their children to adopt wholesome values. By taking their children to Sunday School, where they will learn about Jesus, they can also help them develop worthwhile morals, something most people see as valuable.

- Emphasize the low cost. It is not costly to attend a free and conveniently scheduled class or session, read a pamphlet, or watch a video that promises to be valuable. (We must be clear, however, that true discipleship is costly.)

- The ultimate benefit is giving up ourselves to receive eternal life.[3] Discipleship costs us dearly but yields unimaginable rewards both in this life and beyond.[4] If we can communicate something of the wonder of what is to be gained, what we have to give up will seem like a pittance! On the other hand, if we understand the futility of life as Solomon did in Ecclesiastes, it may not seem such a great sacrifice to give up our life to God's purposes!

Emphasize that the idea you are presenting has benefits far outweighing the costs.

Compatibility

How consistent is the new idea with the person's values and beliefs? If the idea you are presenting fits in well with the person's beliefs, it is easier to adopt. Rogers illustrates the point by telling the story of a remote tribe who would not adopt a more productive type of corn seed because they believed the earth only provided a certain amount of good, and if they got more, their neighbors got less. Getting a better crop was incompatible with their beliefs.

Present your idea as much as possible so that it will fit in with ideas and techniques the audience already holds.

It helps if the new idea is also compatible with their habits and techniques. I was once involved in helping a printing company computerize their accounting. Their procedures were remarkably archaic and inefficient, being done on complicated forms by hand. There were excellent "off the shelf" accounting packages available, but they were not willing to use these. Instead, they paid for expensive, custom software so the screen would look like their inefficient paper forms!

Adopting a new idea sometimes brings consequences you might not foresee. I once had neighbors who were very pleasant, but when I tried to invite them to church or to tell of my faith, they were highly resistant. I finally found out they were Catholics who didn't practice their faith because they had a strong disagreement with the church over birth control. Yet they wouldn't even consider going to a Protestant church because that would be offensive to their Catholic parents.

In our evangelistic efforts we sometimes urge people to "only believe." I think this is fundamentally dishonest. What we are asking is not easy. Jesus taught that becoming His disciple would totally revolutionize our values. Our belief affects every aspect of our lives. We can expect to endure some difficulties as a result.[5]

While real incompatibilities should not be overlooked, we can work to minimize some apparent incompatibilities. Over the years Christians have built up a jargon of religious terms not well understood outside the church, and often not easily understood within it. Our traditions may seem quaint or even bizarre to outsiders. Here are some ways we can work to reduce this unnecessary incompatibility.

- Play up common values. At root most non-Christians hold at least some Christian values. Our country, after all, was founded on biblical principles. Research shows 90 percent of Americans still believe in God,[6] and most people say they pray. While religion has less influence in most people's lives than it once did, many non-Christians still have a God-consciousness. If we can appeal to the spiritual consciousness people already have, our message will not seem so strange.

- Learn to speak standard English when talking about religious matters. Avoid words like *salvation, saved, sanctification, holy, fellowship,* etc.

- The more that Christian activities can be made to fit in with the lifestyle of non-Christians, the more effective we will be with them. For example, some churches schedule services at less obtrusive times than the traditional midday Sunday time. A Friday or Saturday evening service or early or late Sunday service allows families to spend the bulk of the day in family activities.

- For many non-believers, religious trappings such as organ music, archaic language ("thee" and "thou"), vestments and robes, etc., may seem strange. Worship forms that use kneeling, raising hands, saying "amen," and going forward to the altar may cause uncertainty and even fear. Asking visitors to stand can cause terror.

Services that seem more like other gatherings people have attended will be more compatible with the expectations of non-believers and cause them to feel less apprehensive. It helps, too, if group activities can be explained first. A printed program can relieve anxiety by letting people know what to expect. Words should be provided for all hymns and choruses. Bible references can include the page number for Bibles that are available in convenient racks.

Simplicity

Ideas that are simple to understand and implement are easier to adopt than concepts that are confusing and hard to use. Sometimes we make religious principles seem unnecessarily difficult by the language we use. We should use Jesus as a model. He used plain, ordinary (not religious or scholarly) language, and often presented deep theological principles in simple stories about everyday life.

Present new ideas as simply as you honestly can.

We should also present only the level of complexity necessary for people at their stage of spiritual development. Paul warned Timothy[7] to stay away from "godless chatter and the opposing ideas of what is falsely called knowledge." He also warned Timothy to avoid myths and endless genealogies.[8]

Paul wrote to the Christians at Rome, "Accept him whose faith is weak, without passing judgment on disputable matters."[9] I would put in the category of "disputable matters" many of the beliefs that divide Christians. There are many interesting and important doctrines mature Christians can discuss endlessly, but it is counterproductive to expose non-believers or new Christians to unnecessary complexity.

Cost of Trying

If an idea can be tried without much cost or commitment, it is more likely to be adopted. A common marketing strategy with food and drugstore items is to give a taste, a free or low-cost sample, or discount coupon. Marketers believe if you will just try their product, you will like it! Car commercials usually suggest that you take a test drive. It's a small, easy step that doesn't cost anything.

Make it easy for people to try out your new idea.

Can faith in Christ be tried? Well, yes and no. Psalm 34:8 says, "O taste and see that the LORD is good," but Hebrews 6:4-6 indicates that if people have "tasted of the heavenly gift and have been made partakers of the Holy Spirit . . ." it is impossible to renew then again to repentance if they fall away.[10] I would interpret this to mean there is one level at which people can try or "taste" faith in God and another level at which this is not possible.

Perhaps the distinction can be made clearer by comparing faith in God to marriage.[11] Outside of marriage a man and woman can get to know each other well, to love and care about each other, and even live together and have sex, although this is clearly against God's will. Yet none of this is the same as marriage because the man and woman do not have a legally binding long-term *commitment.*

Commitment, strangely, is liberating because it says, "I'm accepted. I'm no longer on trial. I no longer have to prove myself." Lifetime commitment, not sex or compatibility or even love, is the essence of marriage. A trial marriage is a contradiction in terms!

In the same way a non-Christian can learn many things about God, can pray, and even receive some of God's blessings; however, this is not the same as making a forever commitment to God. Perhaps the prime reason why God hates divorce[12] is because it undermines marriage as a picture of our mutual commitment with God.

To carry the marriage analogy further, we need to recognize there is a "courtship" period before a person is ready to make a full commitment to God. This courtship involves getting to know each other (although God already knows us very well) and gradually learning to trust. Here are some ways we might try to make faith "tryable."

■ Ask people to take small steps of faith. These can include such activities as asking God for guidance, attending a Bible study group or church service, reading part of the Bible, reading Christian literature, watching a Christian video, and listening to Christian music.

■ Avoid pushing too hard. My wife and I taught a singles Sunday School class a few years ago. We noticed several members of the group were so anxious to get married that they would sometimes pursue attractive visitors so vigorously they would be scared away. The same can be true in the "courtship to Christ." Give people time to "try before they buy."

Visibility

New ideas that are visible or can be easily communicated to others are more likely to spread than those that are hidden. If you drive through states like Minnesota, you can see test plots for various brands of hybrid corn seed. These are placed next to major highways so everyone who passes can see which corn is doing better.

Some innovations are very difficult to observe or even discuss. For example, vasectomy is a highly effective and convenient form of birth control, but there is no observability and little talk about it, so it has not caught on widely.

Try to make your idea observable.

Christianity is supposed to be observable. The Pilgrims came to the New World to establish a testimony, "a city built on a hill." The Hebrews were God's chosen people not only for their own benefit; they were also God's vehicle for communicating to the world.[13] As Christians, we are God's special instrument at the present time. We are commanded explicitly to preach and witness the Good News in every part of the world.[14]

In my lifetime I have seen two trends that have interfered greatly with our mandate. The first trend was our reaction to attacks from outside, especially theological modernism and Darwinism.[15] I think the damage was not so much from the attacks but rather from our unfortunate response. We adopted what some have called a "fortress mentality," and withdrew from the public debate. We retreated in doubt and fear instead of courageously taking the intellectual and moral battle to the front lines.

During this time there was an overemphasis on separation. I remember many sermons on, "Come out from among them, and be ye separate."[16] The overemphasis on separation led to a kind of legalism, in which Christian groups were defined by what they were not permitted to do. While we need to be distinct from unbelievers and pure in our behavior, if we overdo separation, we will have little impact on the world.

As a result of our withdrawal, we have separate Christian school systems, publishing houses, bookstores, mental health clinics, broadcasting studios, and recording labels. These are all needed and beneficial, but not at the cost of our withdrawal from the mainstream of society.

While Christians have been withdrawing, secular institutions have become dominated by non-believers to the point where some have become quite hostile to Christians and godly values. In graduate school I several times witnessed open hostility against Christian principles in classes I was taking. It has been well publicized that the "cultural elite" who control the media have values greatly at odds with Christianity.

I'm encouraged that there is a strong movement among young Christians today to recapture the culture of our country.

Over the years I have been teaching radio, television, and film I have seen an increasingly large proportion of the best graduates go into secular broadcasting and film. They are not doing this to avoid religious broadcasting but to have a positive influence on the world by influencing secular media.

Another recent trend that alarms me greatly is that many evangelicals seem to have become so concerned about making a "comfortable" living that they have little energy or inclination for ministry. Young couples can no longer enjoy the standard of living their parents did with only one person working outside the home. As a result, time that women used to be able to volunteer for church work is now consumed with making a living.

On top of this, many young people have been damaged by societal and family factors such as child molestation, divorce, and substance abuse. Our disobedience as a culture to biblical principles of sexual purity is taking a dramatic toll on the energy and resources of the church. We have so many seriously hurting people within our groups that it is becoming harder to minister to those outside.

Here are some ideas to help make faith more observable.

- Intentionality. Because of our scriptural mandate to be a witness, we are obligated to do so. To be effective we must make being "observable" a deliberate purpose of our lives.

- Integrity. If my actions don't agree with my words, my testimony is of no use.

- Boldness. To avoid being hypocritical, I am tempted to be quiet about my faith. I sometimes fear I will be embarrassed because I can't give a good defense. Boldness comes more easily when I live a consistent life and know I have done my homework in preparation. Yet, I am never entirely consistent in my life, nor do I ever feel I have all the answers. So some part of boldness comes from pure faith, willingness to take a risk, and obedience.

Change Is Harder Than We Think

While in graduate school at Michigan State University, I had the privilege of taking a course in diffusion from Everett Rogers. Near the end of the course Dr. Rogers observed that we tend to underestimate what a difficult thing we are asking when we ask people to change. I still remember how he illustrated the point.

Realize change is hard!

First he told us that insects were a good source of protein, and that they are a regular part of the diet in parts of the world. Some people, though, would literally rather starve to death than eat insects. He hoped that we would not be so foolish. I thought to myself I would certainly be willing to eat insects if my life depended on it.

Next, he opened a can of worms. A *literal* can of worms. He passed one to each of us. He pointed out that the worms were cooked, were perfectly sanitary, and even tasted OK.

I looked at that worm in front of me, and thought, *Maybe death wouldn't be so bad! No,* I argued with myself, *This is nonsense. I can eat the worm. How bad can it be.*

So I ate the worm. It wasn't that bad, but I did feel a little queasy.

I understood his point. It is a small thing to eat a worm, but it is different from my traditions and experience.

Let's not underestimate what a difficult thing we are asking when we ask someone to change!

Chapter Summary

New ideas spread in a predictable way—slowly at first, then more rapidly as more people hear about it. The first people to try out a new idea are too different from most of the people in the community to be very influential. The most influential people are the early adopters—respected in the local community, usually a bit wealthier, and more educated and progressive than the average. The last people to adopt ideas often do so late, after any benefit they might have gained has disappeared.

Some new ideas catch on earlier than other ones. If a new idea seems to have a high relative advantage, fits in well with other ideas and practices, is easy to understand and execute, and can be tried with only minimal cost, it is more likely to be chosen.

1. See Everett M. Rogers and F. Floyd Shoemaker, *Communication of Innovations*, 2nd ed. (New York: Free Press, 1971) for an excellent and very readable summary of research in the field of diffusion.

2. Adapted from Rogers and Shoemaker, 183–85.

3. Jesus makes this point powerfully in two parables, The Treasure Hidden in a Field and The Pearl of Great Price. See Matthew 13:44-46.

4. See 1 Corinthians 3:10-14 and 9:25.

5. See, for example: Luke 12:51-53; 2 Thessalonians 1:4; James 1:12.

6. James Patterson and Peter Kim, *The Day America Told the Truth* (New York: Plume, 1992), 199.

7. See 1 Timothy 6:20-21.

8. See 1 Timothy 1:4-6.

9. See Romans 14:1.

10. Quotes from the *New American Standard Bible* (NASB). I realize the Hebrews passage has several possible interpretations.

11. A comparison that is frequently made in Scripture. For example, see Ephesians 5:23 and following.

12. See Malachi 2:16.

13. See, for example: Genesis 26:4; Exodus 34:10; Isaiah 42:6; and Galatians 3:8.

14. See Matthew 28:19-20; Mark 16:15; Luke 24:47-48; John 20:21; and Acts 1:8.

15. A most helpful book on this topic is *Darwinism on Trial*, by Phillip Johnson, (Downers Grove, Illinois: InterVarsity Press, 1993).

16. See 2 Corinthians 6:17, KJV.

Make Yourself Understood

CHAPTER ELEVEN

Know How to Use
Words and Sentences

There are many ways a person can convey meaning to another. A look. A shrug. A way of dressing. A scent. But one particular means is so overwhelmingly important we almost ignore the others. I'm talking about the use of words — verbal communication.

When John spoke metaphorically about the coming of Jesus, he did not call Him God's gesture, or God's scent, he called Him "the Word."[1] Adam's first job in Eden was to name the animals, that is, to create language.[2]

What is a word? It is a sound, or a written representation of a sound, that has meaning. In what sense can a sound "have" meaning? The meaning is not *within* the sound[3] but is associated with it. We *learn* to associate a particular sound with an object or action. The meaning is the *learned* association between the word and what it stands for.

Words are easy to move. The fact that the word is not the same as the thing it refers to gives it great power. Take the word *elephant.* I can represent a huge animal with just a tiny bit of ink. I can slip the word into an envelope and mail it anywhere

179

on earth. Let's see you do that with the real thing! The word *forest* conveys the idea of many trees. You can move the word at the speed of light by using a telephone, but you can only move a real forest with a huge amount of heavy equipment and expense.

Words often last longer than the things they represent. Just before Moses died, he strongly cautioned the Children of Israel to take to heart all the words he had given them and to teach them to their children.[4] You and I weren't there when the sea opened to let the Jews escape Pharaoh's army, but we can still take encouragement from the story because we have the words.

We can also use words to talk about the future. Even though I have never been to heaven, I plan to go there. In fact, my life is dominated by the hope of spending eternity in heaven. I have given up some things I might have enjoyed in this life for the sake of the life which is to come. Like the man who discovered a pearl of great value,[5] I feel the little I give up is nothing compared to what I will receive!

What basis do I have for this strong belief in heaven? It is mentioned in 434 verses of the Bible (according to my computer's count). John 3:16 says I may go there if I believe in Jesus. So, my hope is based on *words.*

Truth, Lies, and Errors

But I don't trust *all* words. Because words are not physically attached to the things they represent, they can *mis*represent. If misrepresentation is deliberate, we call it a lie; if it is unintended, we call it an error.

How can I tell truthful words from lies or errors? Unfortunately the words themselves offer little help, except in the case of an inconsistent liar who is not able to keep his story straight. In some cases we can verify the truth of the words by looking at the object described. But, for the most part we have to consider the reliability of the source. The reason I believe heaven exists is not just because I want to, or someone says it does, or I have been there. I believe because the *Bible* says heaven exists. After much thought and careful examination, I have come to the conclusion that the Bible is reliable; therefore, because the Bible tells me there is a heaven, I believe it.

As Christians it is not enough to simply avoid lying. We must intentionally tell the truth. Many who would not lie are still careless about the truth. Passing on a rumor is a good example. Willing ignorance is another.

As a young missionary sailing on a freighter to my first overseas assignment, I engaged an elderly man in conversation with the intent of sharing Christ with him. In the course of our conversation he brought up the nature of the Jewish religion, and I proceeded to tell him what Jews believe. As I pontificated, I noticed his wry smile gradually expand into a full grin, and only then did I realize I was telling a Jew about Jewish beliefs, a topic I actually knew very little about.

> **Ethical Point**
> It is not enough to avoid lying. Christians need to tell the truth!

How embarrassing! My ignorance was exposed. How much better it would have been if I had just confessed my ignorance early. Then I could have spent some time learning about the Jewish religion.

To be willingly ignorant when the truth could be known is a sin of omission just as lying is a sin of commission.[6] The root of such foolishness is pride which leads to unwillingness to admit ignorance or to seek the wisdom of God or others.

Words have enormous power for good or evil. God confused the language at Babel to limit the potential for evil that having a common language provided.[7] God is very concerned about how we use words and has given strong warnings about misusing them. Two of the ten commandments, not misusing the name of the Lord, and not bearing false witness, bear directly on use of language. The Bible has many appeals for telling the truth and not lying.[8]

It is my conviction that far too many Christians treat truth carelessly. Some exaggerate routinely. We think nothing of telling "a little white lie." We cover up inconsistencies in our life-style with lies from our lips. Some of our church leaders are so given to stretching the truth that the cynical expression, "speaking evangelistically," was born. Christian institutions have been known to pad the truth in their advertisements.

As strange as it sounds, some Christians even deceive on behalf of God. When I was a student at a Christian college, we were to have a testimony time around a campfire one evening. Another freshman suggested that we run a thin wire, which would be invisible in the darkness, from a tall building nearby into the fire pit. Then one of us would encourage the group to pray that God would send fire, while the other would light some gasoline-soaked rags and slide them down the wire. He felt this would be a great stimulus to the faith of the students! What a small god this student must have had to think the Almighty could benefit from trickery.

Others lie for God in more subtle ways. These modern day followers of "Job's comforters,"[9] maintain that because God is just, any troubles we encounter must be due to our own rebellion, unconfessed sin, lack of faith, etc. They seem to be willingly ignorant of the many warnings and examples in Scripture that the righteous will have hardships in this life.[10]

Fiction and Falsehood

Words can also be used to convey what is not and could never be! Creative genius Stan Freberg once did a radio spot in which he transformed the Great Lakes into hot chocolate with marshmallows dropped by the Royal Canadian Air Force. One of my favorite storytellers (he calls himself a liar) is Garrison Keillor, with his stories about the mythical town of Lake Wobegon, Minnesota.

Stories that are not true often convey truth very effectively. The Narnia stories of C.S. Lewis never cease to amaze me with the depth of spiritual insight they convey. I read Nathaniel Hawthorne's *The Scarlet Letter* in college, and it served as a strong warning: "Be sure your sins will find you out!" Even a situation comedy on television can sometimes communicate profound truth.

But, is it wise to use what is not true to convey truth? Most of us see no problem with this, but some do. For example, British humorist Malcolm Muggeridge became a Christian in his later years, and gave a series of talks at the BBC which were reproduced in book form.[11] He argues that television is so pervasively fictional and false that it is not a suitable medium for truth. He maintains viewers won't be able to distinguish what is true from what is not.

He has a point. Certainly much fiction is full of sex, violence, and anti-Christian values. Christians need discernment. I do not argue with those who get rid of their television sets.

But suppose we accept Muggeridge's argument and do not use television or other predominantly fictional media to present the truth. That will only decrease the amount of truth available to the average person. Instead, I believe we should take every opportunity to present the truth by every means available.

I see the media as being like the marketplace of old. It is the place where all kinds of ideas are voiced, and where merchandise is sold. Jesus astonished the religious people of his day by taking his message out into the marketplace. I believe we should do the same.

Words in Groups

Words are vastly more powerful because they are part of a system of symbols we call language. Animals can be trained to respond to certain isolated sounds, but when you start linking words together in strings, you soon reach the limit of their ability to respond appropriately.

The ability to combine words increases their utility. The phrase, "big, yellow house," combines three concepts, narrowing meaning, becoming more specific. (See the diagram.) The yellow circle includes all things yellow. The big circle includes everything that is big. The house circle includes all houses. The area where all three overlap would include all big, yellow houses.

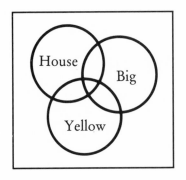

When we combine words we follow rules. The phrase could be "big, yellow house," or "yellow, big house," but not "yellow, house big," for example. Just as we learn the words (vocabulary) we also learn the rules (syntax or grammar). We learn the rules so well, in fact, that we often follow them habitually although we couldn't state them. We know that sentences are divided into subjects and predicates made up of parts of speech such as nouns, pronouns, adjectives, verbs, and adverbs. But when we use language, we usually don't have to think about the rules of grammar.

The amazing ability of the human brain to form thoughts into language is not yet very well understood by scientists. Think of the complexity. The person must select from a vocabulary of perhaps tens of thousands of words just the right one that conveys the desired nuance of meaning, then combine that word with a continuing stream of others in a way that obeys the rules of grammar, and all at more than 100 words per minute. That is far beyond what even the most powerful computers can do, and this is from a small, lightweight device that runs on sugar. I don't have enough faith to believe anything as marvelous as the human brain could have happened by chance!

Fortunately, we can understand each other fairly well even when we make grammatical errors. One study[12] found that adding errors in grammar to written communication did not affect learning, but did adversely affect people's opinion about the competence of the source.

Avoid grammatical errors. Even if people understand you, they won't be as likely to believe you.

When I started teaching college, I was worried that students would challenge my ideas and expose my incomplete knowledge. So, I spoke defensively, more to impress than to inform. But I found that only a few students will challenge a professor. (It's so rare I actually enjoy it when it happens.) The unexpected problem I faced was that the students didn't even *understand* much of what I was saying. I might as well have been speaking Greek.

I came to realize that over the years my vocabulary had grown. During the four years I was in graduate school most of my conversations had been with professors and other graduate students. I had learned many new terms and concepts, but then I forgot that I *learned* them. Once I knew the terms, it seemed as if I had always known them, and it seemed almost impossible to communicate without using them. It was hard for me to understand that the freshmen I was teaching had no clue as to what I meant! I had become exactly what I had determined I would never be – a stuffy professor who used stilted language!

Well, I had to break out of that! But how? The work of Rudolph Flesch provided guidance. After examining many formulas, some of them very complicated, he discovered he could best predict if something would be easy to understand by looking at just two factors, the length of the words and the length of the sentences. If you use short words and short sentences, people will understand you!

Use short words and short sentences.

Most of us have no trouble being understood in ordinary conversation. "Hi. How are you? Did you have a good weekend? We went for a drive in the country. The wildflowers were blooming." These are all short sentences, with short, familiar words.

But something weird happens when we sit down at a typewriter or computer.

Greetings and felicitations as to the universal vivacity and well-being of you, your brood, your spouse and/or significant other which, being an initiatory assertion of no great repercussion, nonetheless obligatory in such circumstances, but requisite as precedent to more pivotal fraternization, to be followed in due season by interrogation about the preceding multi-day time frame in which you may have had (or may not have had) occasion for recreational or other non-obligatory exercises.

In writing and formal speech we tend to shift into the mode of using long sentences and big words that are hard to understand. The cure? Make your writing and speech more like simple conversation. Use the **KISS** formula—Keep It Short and Simple.

Vocabulary Diversity

Vocabulary diversity is the extent to which a communicator uses different words and avoids repetition. In one study[13] it was found that vocabulary diversity caused the source to be seen as more credible. Another found it aided comprehension.[14]

English is an immeasurably rich language with many parallel words of similar meaning, each with a slightly different nuance or color. A computerized thesaurus can be a great help in finding words with better fit to the meaning and greater appeal to the eyes and ears of the reader.

Chapter Summary

Words are extremely important as means for communication, but they can also be used for deception or to communicate error. It is not enough for Christians to avoid lying intentionally. We must also do the hard work to discover and tell the truth.

Truth can sometimes be illustrated through the use of fiction, but the danger is that some may have trouble discerning what is true and what is not.

Words become more powerful when used in groups, but rules of grammar must be followed or confusion may result. If you make grammatical errors, people are less likely to trust you. To be easily understood, use short words and short sentences.

1. See John 1:1.
2. See Genesis 2:19-20.
3. There are a few exceptions, called onomatopoeia, in which the word sounds something like the idea it represents. For example, *bang, cuckoo.*
4. See Deuteronomy 32:45-47.
5. See Matthew 13:46.
6. The Bible contains many admonitions against such willing ignorance. See especially Romans 2:18-23, and also Proverbs 10:8, 15; 14:16; and 18:2.
7. See Genesis 11:1-9.
8. See, for example: Deuteronomy 19:16-19; Psalm 63:11; Proverbs 19:9; Acts 5:1-10; Revelation 21:8, 27; 22:15.
9. See the book of Job. The central part of the book is made up of the friends of Job trying to convince him that his troubles are brought on because of some secret sin, and Job's denials of the same.
10. See, for example, Genesis 50:20; Matthew 5:10-12; Acts 5:41; Phillipians 1:20; and Hebrews 11:26.
11. See Malcolm Muggeridge, *Christ and the Media,* (Grand Rapids: William B. Eerdmans, 1977).
12. R. Spencer, "The Investigation of the Effects of Incorrect Grammar on Attitude and Comprehension in Written English Messages" (Ph.D. diss., Michigan State University, 1965).
13. Tamara Carbone, "Stylistic Variables as Related to Source Credibility: A Content Analysis Approach," *Speech Monographs* 42 (June 1975): 99–106.
14. George Klare, *The Measurement of Readability* (Ames: Iowa State University Press, 1963).

CHAPTER TWELVE
Organize Your Message

Is it effective to scare people out of wrong behavior? Or should you try to entice them into good behavior? Is it better to just ignore counterarguments, or to bring them up and refute them?

Fortunately for us, many researchers have studied these issues, and we can benefit from their findings. Unfortunately, the findings are not always simple or consistent. This is because of the intricacy of the communication process.

To communicate successfully we must first capture and hold the person's attention, then we must be understood, and finally we must offer a strong enough reward or benefit so the person will want to change. In earlier chapters I discussed how to capture and keep attention. This chapter will focus on designing a message to be understood and bring about a willingness to yield.

Drawing Conclusions

After you present your arguments, should you draw a conclusion? Or should you just present the facts and leave the conclusion to the listener? Research[1] shows it is better to state the conclusion explicitly. Advertising practice bears this out. Radio and television ads almost always end with an explicit conclusion calling for action. "So, test drive an Oldsmobile today." This may seem unnecessary, but it works. Why is it important to draw conclusions? It may aid understanding of the message. "So that's what he is getting at!" It may also increase yielding, particularly for people who did not understand the arguments.

Draw conclusions for your messages and recommend specific actions.

Order of Arguments

Let's say you can think of 10 reasons why someone should take a specific action. You believe some of these reasons will seem very agreeable to the listener, and some others might seem quite disagreeable. Which should you put first? Research[2] shows the agreeable reasons should come first.

Generally state arguments the receiver will welcome and agree with first.

Suppose some arguments are stronger than others. Where should you put the strongest arguments? Experiments show that we tend to remember things near the beginning of the message best, things near the end of the message second best, and things near the middle of a message least.[3] Therefore, strongest arguments should be used first or last, where they will be best remembered. If you are calling for a decision immediately after the message, then it might be best to present the strongest

189

argument last so it will still be fresh in the mind at decision time. On the other hand, a strong argument at the beginning may help to organize the listener's thinking and help the following arguments to fit into place.

Use your strongest argument first or last so it will be remembered best.

Refuting or Ignoring Opposing Arguments

Let's say you are talking with a college student who says she is an atheist, and you want to help her understand the arguments for the existence of God. You are aware of several arguments atheists use to support their position. During your conversation would it be best to spend some of your time bringing up arguments that support atheism and refuting them, or would it be most effective to spend all your time presenting arguments for the existence of God?

Over the years several studies have been done on this question, and the findings have changed with the situation.[4] However, the following generalizations have emerged.

- Bring up and refute opposing arguments when you are dealing with controversial topics, especially when the audience may be exposed to those arguments.

- Bring up and refute opposing arguments when the audience is initially against your position.

- Bring up and refute opposing arguments when you are dealing with an intelligent or well-informed audience.

- It is not helpful to bring up opposing arguments when the audience is unaware of them and would not hear them otherwise.

190

Bring up opposition arguments and refute them if the audience is likely to hear them elsewhere.

An added benefit of bringing up opposing arguments and answering them is that it makes the audience more resistant to other opposing arguments they may hear in the future.

Repeating a Message

It is widely accepted in advertising that a commercial will not be very effective until it has been heard or seen several times. Thus advertisers speak of "reach" (the total number of people exposed to the advertisement) and "frequency," (the average number of times each person is exposed). It is more effective to design an advertising strategy so that the same people are exposed to the advertisement several times rather than trying to attract an entirely different audience with each exposure.

This practice is supported by communication research. Zajonc[5] found that repeated exposure to words, musical compositions, and works of art resulted in more liking. But after a while, people have had enough. From that point, increased exposure leads to a decrease in liking.[6]

How much is enough? That's hard to say because it depends on such factors as the complexity and ambiguity of the message, and how much time has elapsed between repetitions. A simple message that can be fully understood and appreciated at the first viewing might cause boredom on its second viewing, while a stimulus-rich, complicated, and ambiguous music video might bear repeating dozens of times. One researcher found that *three* was the optimum number of exposures for a simple message over a short period of time.[7]

An important advertising technique is to make commercials that are appealing when first seen (because they are similar to

191

things we already like) and yet not boring and tedious after repeated viewing. That's quite a trick!

Whatever the situation, it is likely you will be more effective in getting others to act if you repeat your messages a few times over time.

Repeat advertising, music, and short messages. They will increase in effectiveness if they are repeated, but be careful not to repeat them so often they become boring.

Emotional or Rational Appeals?

Communicators frequently discuss whether an emotional or a rational appeal is most effective. I think it's a misleading discussion because emotionality and rationality are not two ends of a continuum, like this:

Emotional--------------------Rational

To make something more emotional does not necessarily make it less rational, and vice versa. A better way of viewing it is like this:

That is, something can be high on emotion and high on rationality at the same time, or low on both, or high on one and low on the other. While we know that either emotional or rational appeals can work with very little of the other, the best results occur when combining the two.

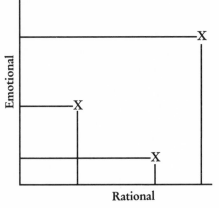

192

While Jesus' sayings are extremely reasonable, I don't imagine they were spoken in a flat, unemotional tone. At times He must have whispered with velvety tenderness and other times roared with potent authority. I think He used the full palette of emotional color on top of a brilliant logical structure.

The degree of emotion should suit the nature of the message. A person who gets too emotional over trivial issues appears silly and out of control. On the other hand, a person who does not show enough emotion appears cold and heartless. I heard someone say you shouldn't talk about hell without tears in your eyes. I like that.

Use strong reason and strong emotion. The degree of emotion should be appropriate to the nature and importance of the message.

Fear

Is the use of fear to motivate attitudinal or behavioral change ethical, and is it effective? In our "enlightened" day we sometimes find the use of fear abhorrent. "How much better to love someone to Jesus than to scare them into the Kingdom."

I believe, however, that fear when correctly used is a very legitimate motivator. It is good and reasonable for people to stop smoking from fear of getting cancer. Many people have changed their sexual behavior from a rational fear of getting AIDS. If a behavior will likely result in harm to the individual practicing it, fear of the outcome is an honest and useful motivation for change.

Fear becomes illegitimate when it is used to suggest a harmful outcome when that is not a reasonable prospect. I read somewhere that a packer of white salmon (instead of the familiar pink variety) printed on the label, "Guaranteed not to turn pink

**Ethical Point
Do not use fear to change behavior when the fear is not morally justified.**

in the can." This implied that pink salmon was spoiled and unsafe to eat. That was an illegitimate use of fear, based on a deception. To create irrational fear is wrong!

It is likewise wrong to play on the irrational fears that many people already have. As a child I was told scary stories about bears by my baby-sitter. The thought of bears still causes my neck hairs to stand up and a cold chill to run down my spine. Likewise, many people hold irrational fears, such as an extreme dread of getting cancer. Some people are irrationally afraid of people of other races. A few are even afraid to go outside. To play on these warped fears is unkind and unethical.

Is fear effective as a motivator? Surprisingly, often it is not. In a classic study researchers found that low levels of fear were actually more effective at changing behavior than were high levels.[8] It may be that the high fear appeals were so terrible that people were not willing to think about them, so they dismissed or forgot them. A high degree of fear works better if the thing that must be done to escape the consequences is easy to do, simple, specific, and can be done immediately.[9]

Researchers found that a high fear message would work under the following circumstances:[10]

- a serious threat is presented;

- audience members feel susceptible to the threat;

- recommendations to control the threat would be effective; and

- audience members have the ability to perform the needed action.

Use fear appeals wisely.

Should Christians use fear to motivate change in belief and behavior? Yes, but it needs to be used with wisdom. The Bible contains many warnings, including the threat of hell (13 verses), but it contains many more references to heaven (434 verses). If you use strong fear, be sure you follow all four of the recommendations above. If at all possible, follow the presentation with an opportunity to take the necessary action at that moment.

Message Organization

All messages have some kind of organization—otherwise the words would just be random. Although it makes sense that well-organized messages would be more effective than poorly organized ones, the research findings have been mixed. Some have not found much difference in comprehension due to organization. Others have found differences in both comprehension and persuasiveness. One researcher[11] found receivers could remember the disorganized content fairly well but that even small amounts of disorganization resulted in less attitudinal change.

Organize your material well.
Poorly organized material may be
harder to understand and less effective
in changing opinions.

There are many ways to organize a message. Bettinghaus[12] suggests several.

- Space. For example, report voting by region.

- Time. Outline the historical development of a situation.

- Deductive. Present a series of statements with which the audience would agree, then present a conclusion which would flow logically from these statements. If these premises are true, then the conclusion must be.

- Inductive. Present an example and apply its principles to other situations. If these principles worked here, they must work everywhere.

- Problem – solution. Outline the problem, emphasizing its severity and urgency, then present the solution and urge action.

Reducing Resistance to Disparate Ideas

If a person receives a message that presents a position similar to one that she holds, it is easy for her to accept the new idea. Or, if the idea is something about which she knows or cares little, it's also easy to accept. But what if she is presented with an idea strongly at odds with core beliefs she cherishes? Then you would expect strong resistance.

Most of us strongly resist the change of deeply held values and beliefs. If we did not, we would be like the person "blown here and there by every wind of teaching."[13] Stability serves us well, unless we are wrong!

Our belief system could be compared to layers of an onion. The deep core beliefs having to do with who we are and our relationships to God and family are at the very center. On the outer layers are peripheral beliefs, not very integral to who we are. For example, I have been using a particular toothpaste for many years, but recently I decided to change. I saw an article in a consumer magazine that said another brand was better, so I'm changing. It was simple. It didn't change my opinion of myself in any significant way.

On the other hand, a few years ago I had to deal with a disappointing truth about a member of my family and my relationship to him. It hit near the core of who I am. It was hard to change my opinion. It required therapy and quite a bit of time.

When we ask people to make changes in strongly held beliefs, we need to expect strong resistance. In some cases we will even see a "boomerang effect." That is, people will become even stronger in their original beliefs.

This idea has long fascinated me, so I chose to study it for my doctoral dissertation. I found that Social Judgment Theory predicted moderate messages would work better than extreme messages in some situations. That is, if you present a message people see as extremely different from their present beliefs, they will be less likely to change than if your message is more moderate. With the extreme message they might even "boomerang" and change in the opposite direction. This effect would only happen if the topic were of great importance to the person.

Extreme changes are more likely to happen over time. Presenting more moderate information first, then gradually working up to the more discrepant information should produce more attitude change.

I tested this idea on college students at the University of New Haven (Connecticut), where I was teaching at the time. I found that marijuana smoking was a topic about which many students felt strongly. I found students who strongly believed in smoking marijuana, and I tried to convince them it is harmful.

I randomly split the students into two large groups. I gave one group four pages of anti-marijuana messages. I gave the other group exactly the same pages, but instead of giving all the information at once I gave them one page a week for four weeks. I started with mildly anti-marijuana information the first week, ending with strong information the fourth week. As predicted, the students who received the messages separated by one-week intervals changed their attitude about marijuana smoking significantly more than those who received all the messages at once.

When we ask people to become Christians, we are asking for an incredible change of many deeply held views. Unless they have been well prepared for this decision, they cannot rationally make it all at once. They must be brought along gradually from where they are all the way to new life and beyond. Remember

> **Give people time to change.
> If you are asking for an extreme
> attitude change in an area very important
> to the receiver, do it in stages.
> First present views the receiver will see
> as fairly close to his original viewpoint
> and then gradually present
> the more disparate views.**

that planting, cultivating, and watering are all necessary prerequisites to harvesting.

Propaganda, Tricks, and the Moral Communicator

Both reason and emotion can be misused by dishonest communicators to distort the truth. Bettinghaus[14] found that students were not very good at detecting logical fallacies but were more likely to believe if something had the *appearance* of being reasonable. But to make something appear to be logical when it is not is deceptive, not a suitable tactic for a Christian. We need to make sure our ideas appear to be sound, and actually are.

Ethical Point
Don't use images to suggest something that is not true. Don't lie through pictures or words.

Advertisers often use images to suggest ideas that would be obviously false if put into words. For example, drinking a certain soft drink does not make you more popular, younger, and better dressed. The honest communicator won't use such techniques to hide a lie.

Dishonest communicators sometimes suggest something is true because others are accepting it. Testimonials are not inherently wrong, but very often they greatly exaggerate the number of people who take a position to give the impression that this "truth" is widely accepted or that the practice is a trend (the "bandwagon" effect). By careful camera placement a tiny demonstration can be made to look like a populist movement.

Further supported by "data" from biased surveys, testimonials can create such a pervasive effect that they can become accepted as a cultural truth. An example is the widely held idea that the majority of teenagers are "sexually active." The moral communicator must stand against such deception.

Years ago a man came to my office and tried to convince me that Christians should use subliminal communication to present the Gospel. Subliminal means presenting messages so they get into the mind without people being aware of it. For example, a message can be flashed quickly on a television screen.

The use of subliminal messages, however, is ethically abhorrent. Presenting information subliminally circumvents people's ability to evaluate and judge the truthfulness of the information. The purpose of ethical communication is to give true information so the receiver can make an informed choice. An ethical communicator respects the right of people to choose and does not try to use force or deception to influence their choices.

> **Ethical Point**
> Respect the rights of others to choose.

Fortunately, the scare of several years ago about the power of "backward masking" and other subliminals seems to have been unfounded. I have not found any research data that shows that subliminals work very well, if at all. Such practices and other forms of deceit certainly must not be used by Christians. Truth, not deception, is our weapon![15]

Chapter Summary

It is more effective to draw specific conclusions and urge action. Agreeable arguments should be used before disagreeable, and strong arguments will be better remembered if they are used either first or last. Generally you should bring up counter-arguments and refute them. A message will be more persuasive if it is repeated often, but people will get bored if it is repeated too often.

Rationality and emotionality should not be thought of as opposites. Your arguments will be strongest if they are both rational and emotional.

Low or moderate levels of fear are usually more motivating than strong levels of fear unless you provide your audience an immediate opportunity to take a simple action to solve the problem.

Poorly organized material will not be as persuasive as well-organized material. If you want to persuade people to believe an opinion that they are strongly opposed to, you will be most effective by delivering several messages over time, with the messages increasing in the degree of difference from the people's original opinion.

Dishonest communicators sometimes use tricks to deceive. These include causing people to think an idea is more popular than it is (causing a "bandwagon" effect), and using photographs that seem to indicate a product will make you loved or popular. Another trick is the use of subliminals. Christians and other ethical communicators should avoid these underhanded methods.

1. C.I. Hovland and W. Mandell, "An Experimental Comparison of Con-clusion-drawing by the Communicator and by the Audience," *Journal of Abnormal and Social Psychology* 47 (1952): 581–88.

2. William J. McGuire, "Order of Presentation as a Factor in Condition-ing Persuasiveness," in *Order of Presentation in Persuasion*, ed. C.I. Hovland, (New Haven: Yale University Press, 1957), 98–114.

3. William McQuire, "The Nature of Attitudes and Attitude Change," in G. Lindzey and E. Aronson, eds, *Handbook of Social Psychology*, 2nd ed., vol. 3 (Reading, Mass.: Addison-Wesley, 1969), 210–11.

4. For an excellent discussion, see McQuire, "The Nature of Attitudes and Attitude Change," 212–14.

5. R.B. Zajonc, "The Attitudinal Effects of Mere Exposure," *Journal of*

Personality and Social Psychology, 8(2), part 2, (1968): 1–27.

6. R.B. Zajonc, H. Marcus and W. Wilson, "Exposure Effects and Associative Learning," *Journal of Experimental Social Psychology* 10 (1974): 248–63.

7. John Cacioppo and Richard Petty, "Effects of Message Repetition and Position on Cognitive Response, Recall, and Persuasion," *Journal of Personality and Social Psychology* 37 (1979): 97–109.

8. I. Janis and S. Feshback, "Effects of Fear-arousing Communications," *Journal of Abnormal and Social Psychology* 48 (1953): 78–92.

9. Howard Levanthal, "Findings and Theory in the Study of Fear Communications," in *Advances in Experimental Social Psychology*, vol. 3, ed. L. Berkowitz, (New York: Academic Press, 1970).

10. Kenneth H. Beck and Adrian K. Lund, "The Effects of Health Threat Seriousness and Personal Efficacy upon Intentions and Behavior," *Journal of Applied Social Psychology* 11(5) (1981): 401–15.

11. D. Darnell, "The Relation between Sentence Order and Comprehension," *Speech Monographs* vol. 30 (1963): 97–100.

12. Erwin P. Bettinghaus, *Persuasive Communication*, 3rd ed. (New York: Holt, Rinehart, and Winston, 1980), 134–40.

13. See Ephesians 4:14.

14. Erwin P. Bettinghaus, *Persuasive Communication*, 3rd ed. (New York: Holt, Rinehart, and Winston, 1980), 144.

15. See, for example, Proverbs 12:17; 2 Corinthians 6:7; Ephesians 6:14.

CHAPTER THIRTEEN

Tap the Power of
Nonverbal Communication

Words are such powerful tools for communication that
we almost forget there are other means sometimes
even more powerful than words.

In defining nonverbal communication we don't have much
trouble with the term *nonverbal,* because it simply means "anything but words." So a tree would be nonverbal, as would a
drop of water, or a kiss. The question is, are they *communication?*

Author David Berlo[1] defined communication as the transfer
of "patterned matter/energy with referent." Patterned matter/
energy is anything that can be perceived by the senses (matter
or energy) and that has some discernible pattern. That would
include virtually anything in the physical realm. The key idea is
"with referent." If something (either matter or energy) *refers* to
something else in someone's mind, communication has taken
place. If a particular tree means something beyond itself to
someone, then it is a symbol to that person. To others, it is just
a tree!

Let's say a friend wants to stop by my house at night to pick up a videotape. He's not sure what time he might come, and doesn't want to wake me if he's late. I tell him, "If the lights are on, I'm up." The lights communicate because they *refer* to the fact that I am up.

But suppose that conversation never took place. He drives by my place after midnight and sees the lights on. He surmises, "The lights are on, so he must be up." Has communication taken place? Yes, according to Berlo's definition. His definition does not say anything about intention to communicate or share meaning with another person.

Let's continue our story. My friend rings the bell, and I jolt awake, fumble around trying to find a robe and my glasses, waking my wife. I struggle downstairs on rubbery legs, and crack open the door.

"Oh, I'm sorry. Did I wake you? I saw the lights and thought you must be up."

"That's OK," I mutter. "I left the lights on for my daughter."

In this case my friend received some information—my lights were on—and wrongly interpreted it. He assumed intent to communicate on my part, but I had no such intention to communicate with him.

This story illustrates a weakness of nonverbal communication. When someone speaks, you are fairly sure he intends it. If he says it in a language you know, you have some confidence you understand his meaning. In a nonverbal situation you are much less sure about the meaning, and if he intended any meaning at all.

Consider the following situation. You are walking into church and see a friend. Just as you are about to greet her, she turns and walks away, saying nothing. What do you make of it? Maybe she didn't see you and suddenly remembered something she needed to do. Maybe she saw you and didn't want to talk to you, but didn't realize you had seen her. It could be that she saw you and knew you saw her and wanted you to know she is upset with you. It could be . . . a thousand different things. We often read a meaning into such encounters that is far different from the intended meaning.

With nonverbal communication, I could communicate something either intentionally or unintentionally, and you could receive it believing I either intended or did not intend to communicate. I might wear a red shirt because it was the only clean one I had (no actual intention to communicate). You might guess that I wore it because I wanted you to notice me (attributed intention). On the other hand, I might have worn the shirt to get your attention (actual intention to communicate). You might have assumed I wore it for another reason (no attributed intention to communicate).

Because nonverbal behavior is harder to control than what we speak or write, we may give off meaning we don't intend. In my high school days when I was around girls I tried to act cool. But my sweaty palms always gave me away. How can you act casual when your hands are dripping sweat?

The difficulty in controlling nonverbal behavior can be an advantage for the receiver. When my kids were little, it used to amaze them that I could tell when they were lying. It wasn't hard. They could control their words pretty well, but their shifty eyes and unsteady voices gave them away. Most people learn to lie better as they get more experience, but even so we can often see some telltale signs.

Nonverbal communication is not necessarily intentional. We cannot live without giving off some kind of impression. Even the absence of expected behavior communicates. We are always communicating something, whether we wish to or not. To some extent we can choose what we communicate, but we cannot choose not to communicate at all!

Nonverbal communication is also more likely to be emotional than rational. While it's possible to give arguments without words, it's difficult unless you are using word-like symbols, such as sign language. Nonverbal signals often tell us how someone is *feeling*, whether they like or dislike something, if they are calm or excited, happy or sad. Ignoring nonverbal signals will often cause you to misinterpret what is being communicated.

Pay attention to nonverbal behavior. It will give you information about how to interpret the words.

Often the feelings are the most important part of a discussion. I ask a friend how he is doing. He says, "OK," in kind of a tentative way, with a sigh. If I hear only his verbal response, I have missed the thrust of his meaning.

Facial Reactions

Is a smile a universal language? Well, yes and no. Researchers have found that people all over the world understand both the nature and intensity of facial expressions. However, there are different rules about when it is appropriate to show them.[2]

When I was living in Japan, an American military woman hired a young Japanese woman to help as a maid around her house. One day when the American woman returned after shopping, the maid presented her with the pieces of a broken dish carefully wrapped in a napkin.

It was not a particularly important dish, and the American would not have been bothered about it except for one thing— the maid thought it was *funny* that she broke the dish. She actually began to giggle. This irritated the American, who lectured the maid on the need to be more careful. The maid giggled even more. By now the American was really getting angry. The confrontation ended suddenly when the maid ran out of the house, never to return, not even to collect her pay.

What happened? The Japanese woman became so painfully embarrassed she could never face the American again. What the American woman did not understand was that among Japanese women giggling is an acceptable way to express embarrassment.

Apparently all human beings have the same inborn facial reactions to emotions, and we all recognize them. We have also learned to stifle or manage these natural reactions to make them more culturally acceptable. Sometimes we are only partially successful in controlling our facial displays, and a careful observer could see some true emotion leaking through. For example, a highly agitated person might be able to control his voice, but not his eyes.

Another form of leakage is "micromomentary" facial expression. These brief flashes, about one-fifth of a second, are too quick to be seen in real time, but can be noticed when film or videotape is played back in slow motion. They are thought to be short lapses in the person's ability to cover the underlying true emotion. While they happen too fast for us to be aware of them, it is possible they may register subconsciously and give us a hunch as to the person's true feelings.

There is some evidence that the same cultural display rules that keep us from showing certain emotions may, to some extent, keep us from experiencing them. One of the ways we "feel" an emotion is the feedback we get from the muscles in our face expressing it.[3] If we interrupt the process of expressing emotions, we don't experience them as strongly.

In the same way, if we deliberately put an emotional display on our face, we experience something of the feeling. Try this. With your fingers push up the corners of your mouth. You experience a weak sensation of happiness. Then pull the corners of your mouth down. You feel a little sad. At least I do.

Communication that stirs the heart emotionally and also challenges the mind will be more effective. Showing appropriate emotions on the face is an important part of being an effective communicator.

Show appropriate emotion.
You will be more effective.

My ancestors came from Britain, where reserve and a "stiff upper lip" are considered virtues; therefore, as a young man I did not find it easy to show emotion. I had to work at seeming natural. Here are some techniques that helped me.

- Think through what you are going to say and identify an appropriate emotion for each part. Pencil that emotion into your notes.

- Identify something in your own experience that caused you to feel that emotion. Think about that experience until you *feel* the emotion.

- Practice reading or ad-libbing from your notes while you experience each emotion you have chosen.

- Try to make your face and body be fully involved in the emotion. During practice even exaggerate the emotion if you can.

- Look at your face in a mirror when you are practicing. Are you letting your emotions get through to your face?

- Give yourself permission to feel and express emotions. They won't carry you away, or make you appear to be weak. They will make you seem more genuine.

- Learn to enjoy your emotions, even the darker ones. Expressing emotion can be deeply satisfying.

- If you have trouble feeling an emotion, fake it. Looking in a mirror, figure out how to put on a facial display that looks right for the emotion you want. Chances are the feeling will follow!

Eyes

Why are the eyes called, "the windows of the soul"? I believe it is because by seeing the eyes we can discover which direction a person is looking. Knowing where a person is looking gives us insight into what he is thinking.

There are few communicative acts stronger than gazing into another person's eyes. It says, in effect, "I see you. I know what you are looking at, and I'm not afraid to let you know that." If the person is a stranger, a direct look may be interpreted as a hostile act, a stare.

If the person is a friend or lover, a gaze may be interpreted as a very intimate, vulnerable act. It says, "I like looking at you, and I don't care if you know it." (Of course, it could also be misunderstood as critical or hostile.) The one looking away first may care the least, therefore have less to lose so have more power in the relationship. Devoted lovers sometimes maintain a mutual gaze over a long period of time, since neither wants to signify, "I care less than you do."

For most ordinary communication, an unbroken stare is too powerful. Yet if we don't look the person in the eye at all, we will be perceived as evasive and not trustworthy. We must employ a pattern of looking into the eyes, looking away, then looking back. We also use this pattern as a means to regulate turn-taking in speech. A fairly typical pattern might be as follows. Bob and Krista are having a conversation, and we are watching their eye behavior.

We see here that eye behavior has two functions, the most important being to regulate the flow of conversation. Each knows when to speak because of a look from the other at the end of a sentence. People look away while they are thinking in order not to be distracted. This also communicates to the other person, "Please don't interrupt me now, I'm thinking."

But we also see that Krista interpreted Bob's looking down during her speech as lack of agreement, to which she responded verbally.

As you can see this "dance of the eyes" is highly choreographed. We learn the patterns of eye behavior as we learn language, and like the rules of grammar we know them so well we are scarcely aware of them. Still, there may be room for improvement.

- Make sure you look the person directly in the eye. Looking near the eye makes you seem less sincere.

Verbal	Bob's Eye Behavior	Krista's Eye Behavior
Krista: Bob, do you think we should start a media production	looks to Krista as she starts speaking	looks at Bob when she says his name, then glances away for a few moments as she thinks for a moment
company?	after her question he glances away for a few moments as he thinks	looks at Bob at the end of her question and continues to look at him
Bob: I don't know.	looks at her as he finishes, indicating that's all he has to say for now	
Krista: Well,	looks at Krista	at the end of the word, looks away, thinking.
I was thinking if we pooled our resources and lived very		looks at Bob, beginning on word *pooled*
frugally . . .	glances down	looks at Bob
Uh . . . you don't like that?	after a beat, looks at Krista	
Bob: Well, I . . .	glances back down to think	looks at Bob intensely, waiting for an answer
(after a moment) I'm just not sure the economy is strong enough . . .	looks up on word *economy*, continues looking	

■ Increase your eye contact. Those with more eye contact seem more active, attractive, friendly, confident, sincere, and mature while those with less eye contact appear to be cold, pessimistic, defensive, and immature.[4]

■ Be aware of cultural differences. One study found African-Americans less likely to look others directly in the eye, which causes others to judge them as uninterested and withholding. Also, because of differences in visual turn-taking behaviors, whites are likely to begin talking before African-Americans are finished.[5]

■ Give your attention to the conversation. Don't be distracted by things on your desk or people in the background.

■ The more you like someone the more you maintain eye contact. Poor eye contact may be read as a dislike for the person. Of course you can err on the other side too. Long, unbroken gazes may suggest romantic interest.

Increase your eye contact when talking with an individual or group.

Sometimes people who have excellent eye contact in interpersonal settings do miserably in public speaking or television situations. Here are some tips.

■ When speaking in public, look directly into the eyes of one audience member for several seconds (through a phrase or sentence), then shift into the eyes of another. Make eye contact with individuals, not just the group en masse. Shift between left and right parts of the auditorium periodically so all can see your face at least some of the time.

■ When speaking on television, first determine if it is appropriate for you to look at the camera or not. If you are part of a panel or are being interviewed, you should look at the interviewer or other panel members, not at the cameras. If you are addressing a congregation or audience, you should look at them as you normally would. In these cases, the television audience members are not being directly addressed, but are eavesdropping on a conversation. If you are addressing the audience directly, however, you must look into the camera lens.

■ Try to look at the lens just as you would look into the eyes of a friend. That is, do not stare continuously, but glance down from time to time, especially when you are thinking.

■ When looking into a camera, look directly into the center of the lens. Looking a little to the left or right makes you seem less direct and sincere. Resist the temptation to glance at a real person standing near the camera. That will make you look shifty.

■ If you must read an "idiot card" on camera, have it held just above the lens. This will open your eye a bit, and is preferable to the more common practice of holding it below the lens. The card should never be held to the side of the lens.

Voice

While it is possible to create vocal sounds apart from words (such as clearing the throat), most vocal sounds accompany words. Their greatest power comes from the ways in which they change the meaning of the words. They can intensify, clarify, contradict, illustrate, or add a whole new level of meaning unrelated to the words.

There are several nonverbal aspects of speech, each of which can be used independently or in combination with others. Here are some ideas of how you can use them.

211

Vary Your Inflection

This is the up and down pitch movement during speech. Pitch variation makes the speech seem more exciting, emotional, and interesting. Raising the pitch for a certain word emphasizes it. Lowering the pitch dramatically at the end of a sentence (except a question) makes you seem more definite and positive.

The importance of inflection can be seen in the little word, *Oh.* With rising inflection it means something like, "Is that really true?" (try it). With rapidly falling inflection it means, "I didn't know that." Slowly falling inflection means, "I am very sorry to hear that." With inflection that first rises then falls it means, "I'm surprised to know that." Inflection that starts and stays low says, "I accept what you say, but I'm not very excited about it." So you can see that inflection has a great deal of power to modify the meaning of speech.

Increase the up-and-down pitch movement of your voice as you speak.

You can't speak without making sound at some pitch. If you don't vary the pitch much, you will sound very guarded, mechanical, and uninterested. If you wish to sound interested and interesting, vary your pitch considerably. (On the other hand, inflection can be overdone. It should seem natural.)

Most of us err on the side of too little inflection. If you are in the habit of speaking without much pitch change, you may need to practice increasing inflection. What seems like exaggeration to you may seem natural to others. A good test is to record yourself, then check for a natural sound when you play back your words.

Speak Faster

Most of us can read several times faster than we can speak. This tells us the brain has capacity to process information much faster than we can talk, so if we increase our speaking rate, we will more nearly match the processing ability of the brain. A slow speaker makes us feel drowsy (too little stimulation to keep the brain active), and we may need to think about other things to avoid falling asleep! Researchers have found that faster speakers seem to have higher intelligence, knowledge, and objectivity, and therefore are more persuasive.[6] On the other hand, too-rapid speech makes you seem nervous.

Speak faster. Faster speakers appear to be more intelligent, knowledgeable, and objective.

Vary Your Speaking Rate

Especially when you are speaking before a group, be aware that audience members may "tune out" from time to time to think about other things. When this happens, your speech becomes background. Any significant *change* in your manner of speaking will tend to bring it to the foreground again. So, speeding up or slowing down your rate of speaking momentarily will help you regain the audience's attention.

Rate changes will also make your material seem more interesting. Paul Harvey, the most popular radio newscaster, often uses extreme rate changes to dramatize and emphasize stories. He sprints through some sentences, then tiptoes thoughtfully, syllable by syllable, through others.

Vary Intensity

You may have seen the television commercial which claims, "If you want to get someone's attention, whisper." It's true. Shouting also works. It's not that shouting and whispering are more powerful than ordinary speech, but they usually reflect a *change*. It is the change in intensity that grabs our attention.

213

Here too, it can be overdone. Too much intensity may make you seem unnatural or manipulative, especially in a small setting.

Vary intensity.
Speak louder or softer
to emphasize a point and gain attention.

Use Pauses

Pauses occur naturally in speech because we must breathe, and we sometimes stop to think about our next words. Pauses also help us as listeners because they serve as a kind of nonverbal punctuation, helping us identify the end of phrases and sentences. Pauses stuck. Awkwardly in the mid. Dle of sentences give the listener somewhat the same sensation you just received.

Use pauses for "punctuation" and emphasis.

A speech that is memorized or read word for word may come across as "slick," largely because it lacks natural pauses. So, put the pauses back in deliberately, especially at the end of thoughts.

Avoid Too Many Nonfluencies

Nonfluencies are the awkward pauses and especially the "uhs" and "ers" that are sometimes called "filled pauses." While some nonfluencies are natural, too many of them will make you seem less competent and powerful.[7] I once had a student tell me after class that I said, "uh," 64 times during the lecture! I worked hard to change. Filled pauses, more than silent pauses, are most likely to make us appear nervous. Inappropriate pauses also make us appear to be lying.[8]

Don't say "uh" or "er" too much.

Pronounce Words Correctly

Generally people will be able to understand what you mean even if you mispronounce (or misspell) quite a few words,[9] but they may have a lower opinion of your expertise.

Learn to pronounce words correctly. People will be more likely to trust what you say.

Overcome Extreme Accents

If people have trouble understanding you, you won't be very effective. People don't want to work hard just to understand the words you are saying.

On the other hand, a regional or foreign accent may add an interesting touch of "class" or a dash of flavor to speech. Billy Graham's ministry does not seem to have been hindered by his distinctly Southern accent. John Kennedy achieved political power in spite of a New England accent. Americans seem to love many of the British dialects.

Some regional accents, however, may be associated with less educated groups of people and may therefore need to be overcome to avoid prejudice.

Develop a Richer Voice

Some voices have full, rich sound, while others seem thin and flat. It is beyond the range of this book to fully address how to develop a rich voice, but here are some tips.

- Breathe from the diaphragm. You can tell you are breathing from your diaphragm if your "stomach" muscles tighten as you speak. Controlling your breath from your chest gives you a thin, breathy sound.

- Avoid a "nasal" sound. This is accomplished by opening the soft palate that divides the mouth and nose so you gain the added resonance of the nasal cavity. You may not be aware that you can control this "trap door." (If you could not close it, you would not be able to blow up balloons because air would leak out through your nose.) Choir directors often trick us into opening the passage up by saying such things as, "Think of the tone as going up high into your head before it comes out," or, "Think of the sound as coming out through your forehead."

- Speak in your best pitch range. There is a particular range in which your voice will be most pleasing, higher for some, lower for others. If you are habitually speaking above or below your ideal range, your voice will sound a bit pinched and artificial.

- Relax. Too much tension will make your voice sound strained and tense. Learning to relax will give you a more pleasant and natural sound.

Hands

Like the face and voice, our hands can be expressive. With our hands we can emphasize a point by "pounding" or "chopping." We can direct attention by pointing, and we can illustrate something by drawing a picture in the air. All of these would generally accompany speech, to strengthen or modify meaning.

We can also create symbols that have wordlike meaning, such as the OK sign, the sign of the cross, a clenched fist, and "come here" and "stop" gestures. The various sign languages used by the hearing impaired, and the system of hand signals used by broadcasters illustrate that one can communicate entirely through gestures.

There is some scientific evidence that we remember more information when a speaker uses gestures.[10] The amount of gesturing people do depends somewhat on the situation (people use gestures more in public speaking situations),[11] and to a large extent on culture. Italians, for example, gesture far more than do British.[12]

Especially in public speaking situations, use gestures freely because they aid learning.

Some movements of the hand may present an unintentional message. For example, I have had a bad habit of playing with small objects (like my watch or paper clips) when I am a little bored. Someone might interpret this as nervousness.

The Body

While the rest of the body is not as expressive as the face, it is harder to control, and thus reveals truth we try to hide. You can probably judge someone's truthfulness best by noticing how the person is sitting. Look for nervous mannerisms and jiggling motions. Does the person shift position frequently?

Posture communicates how we feel. If we're "down," we tend to slump or hunch over. If we're feeling great, we stand more erect. We can tell something about a person's mood when he enters the room, simply by stride and posture. On the other hand, some of us give off incorrect messages through careless posture.

217

Early on, my mother noticed my tendency to slouch, and when I was in grade school, she asked me to look around several times a day and make sure I was sitting straighter than the other children. She was on the right track. When I stand and sit erect, I not only look better but I also feel happier and more confident.

Posture also makes a difference for receivers of communication. Your messages will be more persuasive if your receivers are seated or reclining comfortably.[13] That's probably why car salesmen try to get you to sit down while they work out the deal!

Make sure your audience is seated comfortably. They will be more easily persuaded.

Generally, a person who leans slightly forward with legs uncrossed and arms a little away from the body will appear more open and strong. A person with crossed legs, folded arms, and who is leaning backward will appear more closed and guarded. It would, however, be a mistake to read too much into, say, crossed legs, because this may just be a comfortable position for a certain person.

If people of different status are talking, it would be normal for the higher status person to exhibit a more relaxed posture, while the subordinate would ordinarily be more "at attention." A subordinate who appears too relaxed may not seem to be showing enough respect.

In one-on-one situations with people of equal status, it is common for both to assume a similar body position. When this happens, it indicates liking and equality. Different body positions indicate a perceived difference in status. Researchers also found that when counselors assumed similar postures to their counselees, they were seen as being more understanding.[14]

When counseling, assume the same posture your counselee does.

How you walk also says a lot about you. A strong stride at about two steps a second with arms swinging parallel to the opposite leg, each step landing on the heel and the foot then rocking forward to the toe, head up and gaze straight ahead says you are purposeful and determined. You are also less likely to get mugged![15] A slow saunter, head down, shoulders hunched, says you lack clear purpose and may be vulnerable.

Touching

Touching is one of the strongest forms of communication, partially because it is the first communication form that children learn.[16] Compared to many cultures of the world, Americans don't touch very much. A researcher found that couples sitting in a coffee shop in Puerto Rico touched almost 200 times an hour, French couples touched more than 100 times an hour, while Americans touched only twice. The British, typically, didn't touch at all.[17] We may well be a touch-starved people.

Several studies have shown that both baby animals and humans are healthier if they are regularly touched.[18] It may be that nursing babies is as important because of touching as because of nourishment. Touch is so powerful, in fact, that we have strong societal prohibitions against casual touch.

Touching the sick has often been found to have soothing and healing results, quite apart from any miraculous intervention. It's interesting that Jesus often chose to impart healing through a touch.

Touching is also effective in persuasion. Waitresses who touch their clients on the hand or shoulder when giving change get bigger tips.[19] People who were touched when they were

219

thanked for a small favor were more likely to perform a larger favor.[20]

Touch others when appropriate. Touching is powerful.

Touching is powerful, but the power must be respected. Hugging, and touching on the hands, arms, or shoulders, for example, can be very reassuring and comforting, and should be used when appropriate. Care must be taken that touching does not suggest a sexual invitation.

Clothing

While clothing also serves the needs of protection and comfort, its most important function is communication. How you dress says a great deal about you—the kind of work you do, your aspirations, your age, even your beliefs about sexuality and modesty. Any kind of clothing you wear will give off some kind of meaning. If you wore no clothing at all, that too would have meaning!

That clothing sends a message is well-known in corporate America, where many companies have written dress codes. Others have unwritten codes that are almost as specific.

Clothing is especially important for first impressions. When you want to be seen as competent and trustworthy, you would be well advised to wear a conservative business suit. This is especially true if you are a woman or a young or short man, all of whom have to work harder to be seen as credible.

In one study a model appeared before audiences in five different styles of clothing. She was seen as most "happy, successful, feminine, interesting, attractive, and desirable as a friend" when she wore a formal suit with a blouse. She was seen as having the least of these qualities when she wore jeans and a T-shirt.[21]

Wear a traditional dark business suit with white shirt to appear more knowledgeable and trustworthy.

In some cases, it is possible to overdress, particularly if you are male, large, older, and of higher status when compared to your audience. For example, one researcher found that students viewed teachers in casual clothing as more friendly, flexible, sympathetic, fair, and enthusiastic, while they viewed teachers in dress suits as more organized, knowledgeable, and prepared.[22] Since I am short and looked young for my years when I began teaching, I found it helpful to dress more formally. Now that I am middle-aged, I find students can relate to me more easily if I dress a bit less formally. For example, I will often wear a sweater instead of a suit jacket.

If you are older, larger, and/or of higher status than your audience, they will see you as more friendly, flexible, and enthusiastic if you dress less formally.

Space

As physical beings, we exist in space. The skin forms the outer boundary of the body itself, but we need space beyond this to live and move. The space closest to the body is called "personal space." We maintain and defend this space to feel comfortable and safe.

The amount of personal space varies with the situation from

none at all in a physically intimate relationship, to several feet when talking to strangers. It also varies with culture. I once witnessed a conversation between a Latin American and a North American. As they were talking, the Latin American kept moving closer to the North American because his cultural personal space requirement is smaller. The North American, feeling uncomfortable, kept backing away. Over a period of 15 minutes, the North American backed up 30 feet or more! I can imagine the Latin American thinking to himself, *Why is this guy so standoffish?* The North American might have been thinking, *Why is this guy so pushy?*

Anthropologist Edward Hall identified four categories of distance: "intimate" from zero to about 18 inches; "personal" from 18 inches to about 4 feet; "social" from 4 to 12 feet; and "public," greater than 12 feet.[23] These distances would vary with culture. From these distances and terms you can get an idea of what distance is normal. For example, if you approach a stranger from the front, he or she will become uncomfortable if you get closer than about 4 feet.

Physical closeness intensifies other impressions. An unpleasant confrontation is made even more so if it is close up (getting into one's face). A pleasant conversation might be even more pleasant if the people are close to each other.

Position yourself close to your audience. Your communication will be more intense.

Our "space bubbles" are not spherical. We are more tolerant of people to the side of us than we are of people directly in front. Accordingly, if someone seems too close, I can turn my body so the person is now to my side, and I feel much more comfortable.

In any face-to-face communication, position yourself as close to your audience as is practical.

- Have meetings around a small, round table instead of across a large desk.

- For small classes sit in a circle with the class members to minimize distance.

- If possible, get rid of the lectern or pulpit. It adds psychological distance.

Time

Occasionally, time talks even more distinctly than words. When I was applying for a driver's license in a foreign country, I filled out the necessary forms, took the test, and was told to come back to the same office at 9 A.M. one week later.

I made arrangements for someone to cover my shift and took the long ride to the driver's license office, making sure I got there a few minutes before 9. When I arrived, the same man who had insisted I be there by 9 told me to take a seat, and I would be called when he was ready.

By noon I thought there must be some problem, so I went to the counter again and asked if I should come back again another day. "No," he said pointedly, "Sit down and I will call you when I am ready."

I am not a very patient man, but by now I knew that we were involved in a test of wills. So, I waited. And waited. And. . . .

A little after 5 P.M., after most the staff had left, the man called my name, and I went to the counter. Making sure I saw him, he reached behind him, and picked up my license from a shelf, where I am sure it had been all day!

What was this all about? It was a message about power.

Like most aspects of nonverbal communication, time means different things to different cultures. For some, being an hour or more late for a social engagement or a business appointment is not offensive at all. Others would be very irritated if you were even five minutes late. Being late carries the message, "I'm terribly socially inept and just don't realize how offensive it is when I'm late," or even worse, "I'm so important I can make you wait." Many people who are just careless, or grew up in a culture where time is not very important, inadvertently give off a message of arrogance by being late.

Be prompt for business appointments. Otherwise you may be perceived as a slob or arrogant.

There are also cultural norms of notification if you are to be late. It's said that here in the Los Angeles area you can be excused for being quite late as long as you call from your cellular phone to report that you are tied up in traffic. The nature of the event would also make a difference. If one is attending a dinner party, promptness is particularly important because otherwise the food may be ruined.

In the United States it is generally considered rude to hold a meeting or class even a few mintues over time—regardless of how late it may have started.

Chapter Summary

Nonverbal communication may be less intentional and more emotional than verbal communication. It is often used to tell us how to interpret the verbal message it accompanies. Because it is harder to control, we may be able to judge a person's sincerity through nonverbal behavior.

While faces have nearly universal meaning, expressions do vary with culture. A person showing more emotion will appear more interesting and genuine.

Eye behavior is used to regulate speech. We judge a shifty-eyed person as insincere. A person who makes good eye contact without staring steadily is judged to be more sincere.

Voice factors such as pitch, intensity, and rate help us interpret the words they accompany. We will be more interesting if we vary these factors.

A person with erect or slightly forward-leaning posture will seem more active and interested than a person with slumping posture. Mimicking the posture of the person you are counseling will make you appear to have more empathy.

Touch people when appropriate. Touch is powerful, but must be used appropriately.

To appear more knowledgeable and trustworthy, wear a traditional business suit. Especially if you are older, larger, or of higher status, you may wish to dress down to be seen as more friendly and flexible.

The closer you are to your receiver, the more powerful your message may become. If you are too close, you may seem threatening or overly intimate.

1. David K. Berlo, *The Process of Communication* (New York: Holt, Rinehart, and Winston, 1960).

2. P. Eckman, and H. Oster, "Review and Prospect," in *Emotion in the Human Face*, 2nd ed., ed. P. Eckman, (Cambridge, England: Cambridge University Press, 1982) 178–211. Also see, P. Eckman, "Expression and the Nature of Emotion, in *Approaches to Emotion*, ed. K.R. Scherer and P. Eckman, (Hillsdale, NJ: Lawrence Erlbaum), 319–43.

3. See Silvan S. Tomkins, *Affect, Imagery, Consciousness* (New York: Springer Publishing, 1962), 272–81.

4. R.E. Kleck and W. Nuessle, "Congruence between the Indicative and Communicative Functions of Eye Contact in Interpersonal Relations," *British Journal of Social and Clinical Psychology* 7 (1968): 241–46.

5. M. LaFrance, and C. Mayo, "Racial Differences in Gaze Behavior during Conversations: Two Systematic Observational Studies," *Journal of Personality and Social Psychology* 33 (1976): 547–52.

6. N. Miller, G. Maruyana, R.J. Beaver, and K. Valore, "Speed of Speech and Persuasion," *Journal of Personality and Social Psychology* 34 (1976): 615–42.

7. G.R. Miller and M.A. Hewgill, "The Effects of Variations in Nonfluency on Audience Ratings of Source Credibility," *Quarterly Journal of Speech* 50 (1964): 36–44.

8. R. Krauss, "Improve Your Credibility," *Glamour*, January, 1975, 42.

9. R.J. Kibler and L.L. Barker, "Effects of Selected Levels of Misspelling and Mispronunciation on Comprehension and Retention," *Southern Speech Communication Journal* 37 (1972): 361–74.

10. M.G. Riseborough, "Physiographic Gestures as Deciding Facilitators: Three Experiments Exploring a Neglected Facet of Communication," *Journal of Nonverbal Behavior* 5(3) (1981): 172–83.

11. J.T. Dalby, D. Gibson, V. Grossi, and R.D. Schneider, "Lateralized Hand Gesture during Speech," *Journal of Motor Behavior* 12(4) (1980): 292–97.

12. M.B. Walker and M.K. Nazmi, "Communicating Shapes by Words and Gestures," *Australian Journal of Psychology* 31(3) (1979): 137–43.

13. R.E. Petty, G.L. Wells, M. Heesacker, T.C. Brock, and J.T. Cacioppo, "Effects of Recipient Posture on Persuasion: A Cognitive Response Analysis," *Personality and Social Psychology Bulletin* 9(3) (1983): 209–22.

14. R.E. Maurer and J.H. Tindall, "Effect of Postural Congruence on Client's Perception of Counselor Empathy," *Journal of Counseling Psychology* 30(2) (1983): 158–63.

15. C. Rubenstein, "Body Language That Speaks to Muggers," *Psychology Today*, August 1980, 20.

16. Ashley Montagu, *Touching: The Human Significance of Skin*, 3rd ed. (New York: Columbia University Press, 1986), 97–197.

17. Sidney M. Jourard, "An Exploratory Study of Body-Accessibility," *British Journal of Social and Clinical Psychology* 5 (1966): 221–31.

18. For a fascinating review of the historical background of touching and some case studies in touching in human growth and development, see L.A. Malandro, L.L. Barker, and D.A. Barker, *Nonverbal Communication*, 2nd ed. (New York: Random House, 1989).

19. A.H. Crusco and C.G. Wetzel, "The Midas Touch: The Effects of Interpersonal Touch on Restaurant Tipping," *Personality and Social Psychological Bulletin* 10(4) (1984): 512–17.

20. M. Goldman, O. Kiyohara, and D.A. Phannesteil, "Interpersonal Touch, Social Labeling, and the Foot in the Door Effect," *Journal of Social Psychology* 125(2) (1985): 143–47.

21. M. Harris, J. James, J. Chavez, M. Fuller, S. Kent, C. Massanari, C. Moore, and F. Walsh, "Clothing: Communication, Compliance, and Choice," *Journal of Applied Social Psychology* 13 (1983): 88–97.

22. S. Rollman, "How Teachers' Dress Affects Students' Opinion," *National Enquirer*, Nov. 1, 1977.

23. Edward T. Hall, *The Hidden Dimension* (New York: Anchor Books, 1966).

Foster Agreement

CHAPTER FOURTEEN

Use Persuasion

To get people to do something, you need to capture and hold their attention. You must then present your message clearly so they understand what you want them to do. Next, you must get them to yield, be willing to do what you ask.

Most people are fairly rational. They want to understand what you are asking of them, and what benefits they will receive. People will sometimes be willing to act without understanding, but only if they have a great deal of faith in you or you have some kind of authority over them. Small children have that kind of faith in their parents. Because of authority, an employee might do something an employer asks without understanding the reason.

Sometimes people act on a mere suggestion, with little reflection. We all do this from time to time with trivial decisions, such as buying a candy bar conveniently located near the cash register.

Persuasibility

Some people are more likely than others to be easily persuaded.[1] Children near the ages of eight or nine are more easily influenced than older or younger children or adults. Women are a bit more easily influenced than men, apparently because their superior verbal skills help them understand a message more clearly. People who have moderate levels of self-esteem are more easily influenced than people who have either very low or very high opinions of themselves.

Maybe the following story has a familiar ring to it. Things seemed to be going along pretty well for Joe. Married to a knockout, he had two young sons whom he adored and a successful career selling radio advertising. People at work were impressed with his creativity. Before long he expected to become the sales manager. He and his family had just moved into a beautiful new home which was a bit more than they could comfortably afford, but he was optimistic about the future. He felt quite satisfied with himself. He was not a good candidate for change.

Then, the bottom fell out. The station was sold and the entire staff laid off. He was optimistic at first. With skills such as his he thought he could easily get another job, even a better one. But after six months of interviews he hadn't turned up a substantial nibble. They had to let the house go. They tried to sell it, but the market had gone sour, and it wasn't worth what they owed on it. They peddled their furniture at a garage sale for cents on the dollar. They had to default on their two fancy cars, and bought an old clunker for $300. The most humiliating part was when they had to move in with his wife's parents. The old cockiness was gone. Now he would settle for a job that paid half—even less—than his old one did. Now he was open to new ideas.

With variations this story is the setting for the conversion experience of many, including King Nebuchadnezzar during the time of Daniel.[2] The Bible commends ministering to those who are undergoing misfortune, including widows, orphans, and prisoners.[3] One reason is certainly their great human need, but I believe another reason that people in the middle of stressful times have a greater openness to spiritual reality is because of diminished self-esteem.

Concentrate on people whose self-esteem is at moderate levels, especially those who have had some recent failures.

On the other hand, a person's self-esteem can be too low to be open to new ideas. Betty had a miserable childhood with parents who alternated between ignoring her and abusing her. Plain and painfully shy, she felt she could not compete with the other children in school. She sat as inconspicuously as possible so the teacher would not call on her. The few times she was called on she was so embarrassed she could hardly speak. Classmates thought she was mentally slow, and so did she. Her father dictated all the choices in her life, which was OK with her because she felt unable to make decisions. Before Betty could be won to the Lord or make any other significant decision she must understand that she is a worthwhile person, capable of making good choices.

Persuasion Techniques

Rational people choose to do something because they believe it furthers one of their goals or meets one of their needs. The goal could be selfish or altruistic. For example, people might give to a relief agency such as World Vision because it's important to them that children not go hungry. However, until the need is called to their attention and a way is made for them to fulfill that need, nothing will happen.

Below are techniques for asking people to do something.[4]

Just ask. Many people will respond if you make a clear request.

- "Please do this." The simplest technique is just to ask. People can't read your mind. There are many who would help you, give to your cause, buy your product, or join your class if you asked.

  Salespeople can tell you how important it is to ask for the order. I sold radio advertising for a while, and I was often surprised that when I asked for an order I got it. I was surprised because the merchant had already told me how tough things were and that he couldn't afford to advertise.

- "Do this because." Most people are at least somewhat rational so they are more likely to comply if they believe there is a good reason for doing so. The reason needs to be logical and credible.

  Presenting reasons must be done carefully or you may appear argumentative or more interested in winning the point than in winning a friend. Argumentation should not descend into verbal aggression. People are less likely to yield if they must first admit they are wrong. To admit you are wrong is to confess that in some way you are inferior to the persuader. Most of us hate to do that!

State reasons, but avoid being argumentative. Show respect and care for the receiver.

It helps if the communicator shows great respect for the one he is trying to win over, and tries to keep persuasion in a "win-win" mode rather than an "I win—you lose" mode. If I really believe you have my best interests at heart and that you respect me and care about me, I will be more willing to listen to your arguments. We need to remember that the greatest Communicator of all time came as a servant!

■ "Do this and I'll _____." The basis for much persuasion is to give something to gain something — a fair exchange. If this works correctly, both parties give something of less value to them to gain something of more value — a true "win-win" situation.

For example, a farmer has more food than he needs, so he sells some to acquire money to buy clothing. This is the basis for the entire economic system. Fairness is the issue here.

God's interest in fairness is shown in his requirement of honest weights. A classic way to cheat is to keep two sets of weights, one for buying (heavier) and one for selling (lighter). The Bible condemns this practice,[5] and by implication all methods of misrepresentation.

An exchange does not have to be in the material realm. Parents enjoy lavishing gifts on their children just for the joy and appreciation they receive. They don't expect to be repaid in material things, but they do like it if the children show some sense of appreciation. People give to charity and in return feel good about themselves and feel they have made a difference in the world. Sometimes people give a large amount of money to build a memorial (such as a college building) to themselves or a loved one. That gives them a sense of extending their influence beyond the grave.

■ "Do this *or* I'll _____." This is a threat, which could be either direct or implied. "Pay your electric bill or we'll turn off your power!" This is similar to the above, except that action is taken to avoid a negative result.

■ "Do this because you owe me." Explicit or implied, this appeal for action depends on payment of debt for past favors. Parents may use this tactic on children, and spouses may use it on each other. It may be ineffective if the person being persuaded does not share the persuader's sense of indebtedness. For example, a doting mother cooks meals her teenage daughter does not want, but the daughter eats them to please her mother. The mother may feel the daughter should be indebted to her for cooking the meals, while the daughter may feel the mother is indebted to her for eating meals she did not want.

■ "Do this for me." Most people like to see themselves as kind and helpful, and many will help a stranger who makes an appeal based on need. Recently in Mexico I gave money to a child beggar I will probably never see again. I did not expect to gain anything from the gift—it was a simple response to need. Young men selling magazine subscriptions sometimes come to our door with an appeal like, "I'm trying to earn points so I can go to camp. Can you help me out?"

I would do almost anything my wife asked me to. If she were sick, I would gladly spend all of my money and sell everything I had if it would help her get well. Because I value her highly, her "do this for me" appeal has a great deal more power than the words of a young magazine salesman I don't know.

> ## Build a strong relationship as a basis for making a request. People who value their relationship with you will be more likely to respond to your requests.

Effective fund-raising has sometimes been called "friend-raising." If the potential donor knows and cares little for you or your ministry, the gift, if any, is likely to be trivial. But if the donor knows, cares about, and trusts you and/or your ministry, the gift is more likely to be large. Those who are most successful in getting other people to give and help toward a cause usually have cultivated a large circle of friends.

Many salespeople have learned the value of at least pretending to be your friend. I went car shopping with a friend several years ago, and the salesman used this technique. He pretended he was on the customer's side. He gave the impression that he was risking trouble with management for giving away too much. He suggested my friend make a bid that he said was, "Way too low. They'll never go for it. But what the heck, let's give it a try."

When the bid was approved, he acted as if he had helped my friend get away with robbery. He even threw in a few added goodies which, he said, he would probably get in trouble for. With a friend like that, how could she say no? She didn't.

- "Do this for you." Point out to people the benefits of taking the action you recommend. This is the foundation for much persuasion. People are motivated by perceived benefits to themselves. If the cost-to-benefit ratio is favorable, they buy. Here you can list and explain the benefits and discuss the relative advantage of this choice compared to other choices they might have.

List and explain benefits of your suggestion compared to other options available.

Dealing with Objections

Anticipate and answer objections as much as possible before they come up. You should know the situation of the person you are trying to persuade so that you don't make unrealistic suggestions, and you should give information to answer an objection before it comes up.

Get to the real issue. Sometimes a person will raise a stream of petty objections. When that happens, you can be pretty sure they are just excuses. Try to find out what the underlying problem is rather than wasting time with excuses. Even if you have an answer for every excuse, the person still won't be persuaded unless you have dealt with the underlying issue.

Knowing When to Walk Away

When Jesus gave the Good News to the "rich young ruler," the man rejected the truth and Jesus let him walk away.[6] Ethical communicators must recognize the rights and responsibilities of their audience members to make their own choices. Even when we believe we know better than other people what is best for them, ultimately they make their own choice. We show respect for people by letting them make the choice.

Ethical Point
We must respect other peoples' right to make their own choices.

I like what Campus Crusade for Christ teaches about evangelism: "Take the initiative to share Christ in the power of the Holy Spirit and leave the results to God." We are responsible to present the truth as clearly as we can. What other people do with it is not our responsibility.

On the other hand, it isn't enough to present the truth in a perfunctory, uncaring way. Jeremiah was given the task of warning the people of Israel that if they didn't change their ways, they would be taken into captivity. Even though his message was consistently rejected and he was even put into prison, he gave his message with passion, even tears—thus the title, "the weeping prophet."

Sometimes I am reluctant to take no for an answer because I have defined the "game" in my mind to be "win-lose." If someone says no, I lose. Because I hate to lose, I will try almost anything to get that person to agree with me. In this case, it's not the person I care about, it is myself. I want to win, get the commission, meet my goal, get credit for winning someone to the Lord, or whatever. I may take it as a personal affront if someone rejects my presentation. I end up frustrated and even angry.

Recognize that there are ethical limits to persuasion. The other person must ultimately make the choice.

I'll avoid a lot of frustration, both for myself and the other person, if I remember I'm still OK even if someone doesn't accept my proposal. I am only responsible for my own actions—to present the truth. The other person has the right to choose, and if Jesus Christ Himself did not take that right away, neither should I.

Chapter Summary

People are more easily persuaded if they have a moderate level of self-esteem. Sometimes a failure experience (such as losing a job or getting a divorce) will make a person more open to persuasion.

There are many ways to persuade people. The most basic is to simply ask. In most cases people are more likely to act if they see a clear benefit to themselves and if what you are asking seems reasonable.

As ethical communicators, we must remember that the ultimate choice belongs to the client. We must respect the other person's right and responsibility to choose and not exert unfair influence.

1. For a good discussion on factors affecting influenceability, see William J. McGuire, "The Nature of Attitudes and Attitude Change," in vol. 3 of *The Handbook of Social Psychology*, 2nd ed. Gardner Lindzey and Elliot Aronson, eds. (Reading, Mass.: Addison-Wesley, 1969), 241–52.
2. See Daniel 4:28-37.
3. See, for example, Hebrews 13:3 and James 1:27.
4. A good discussion of compliance-gaining strategies, from which I have borrowed some ideas, is found in Blaine Goss and Dan O'Hair, *Communicating in Interpersonal Relationships* (New York: Macmillan Publishing Company, 1988), 240–44.
5. For example, see Proverbs 20:10.
6. See Luke 18:18-24.

CHAPTER FIFTEEN
Resolve Conflicts

onflict is part of the human situation. It's not necessarily bad. In fact, it can be the stimulus for creative new thinking. All stories, at their root, are about resolving conflict. Conflict is the stuff of the drama of life.

Conflicts are growth opportunities. That's why James said, "Consider it pure joy, my brothers, whenever you face trials of many kinds, because you know that the testing of your faith develops perseverance."[1]

Conflict can improve thinking. If you and I have a disagreement about goals or methods, we may jointly come up with a solution that is better than either of our individual ideas.

On the other hand, conflict is often counterproductive, even destructive. Marriages break up. Churches split. Friendships dissolve. Sometimes people physically assault or even kill others.

The Source of Conflicts

James tells us the root of many conflicts: "What causes fights and quarrels among you? Don't they come from your desires that battle within you? You want something but don't get it. You kill and covet, but you cannot have what you want. You quarrel and fight. You do not have, because you do not ask God. When you ask, you do not receive, because you ask with wrong motives, that you may spend what you get on your pleasures."[2]

External conflicts, then, are the products of internal battles. We prefer to fight for what we want rather than ask God for what He desires to give us. God had already made David fabulously wealthy and powerful as King of Israel and assured him that he would have given him even more.[3] But David took matters into his own hands and stole another man's wife.

As Christians we don't have to steal or lie or beat up other people. God has promised to provide what we need.[4] If He already gave us His Son and the promise of eternal life, will He deny us anything else we need in this life?[5]

We may not always receive what we want or think we need. Paul said, "I have learned the secret of being content in any and every situation, whether well fed or hungry, whether living in plenty or in want. I can do everything through him who gives me strength."[6]

What really bothers me is thinking my "rights" have been denied. I seem to have a strongly developed sense of justice, especially if I feel I am the one not getting it! Several times I have made such a fuss over a minor point that I embarrassed my wife. Jesus didn't behave that way. Though He is God, He gave up *all* His rights for the sake of His ministry on earth.[7] Throughout the Book of Acts His followers were treated very unjustly. They too gave up their rights for the sake of the ministry.

Paul chides Christians for suing other believers. We should instead look to fellow believers to mediate disputes. Instead of filing lawsuits, "Why not rather be wronged? Why not rather be cheated?"[8] As an American I was raised to believe it is good to stand up for my rights. Sometimes it is even better to lay them down.

Jesus taught us to love even our enemies, to "turn the other cheek."[9] Does this mean we are to be "doormats," constantly trampled over by others? Evidently not, for this same Jesus drove the money changers out of the temple.[10] He told His followers just before His crucifixion that if they didn't have a sword, they should buy one.[11]

How do we balance these teachings? I think Paul gives us two keys. He says, "Do nothing out of selfish ambition or vain conceit, but in humility consider others better than yourselves. Each of you should look not only to your own interests, but also to the interests of others."[12] The first key is *humility*, not to see ourselves as more valuable than others. The second key is to seek *mutual interests*, that is, both my interests and your interests.

Avoid conflict through biblical humility and by seeking mutual interests for a "win-win" solution.

Humility

If I see myself as "better" than you, my goals as most important, etc., then I will feel justified in pushing my own agenda at your expense. If I realize I am no more or less important than anyone else, I will value your goals, beliefs, and feelings. Scripture tells us not to think of ourselves more highly than we ought.[13]

It's easy for those of us in ministry leadership to get caught up in a sense of our own importance. After all, what could be more important than being a leader in the work of God? Those around us make the problem worse by pushing special status on us. We accept it. Gladly.

Remember, in God's eyes you are no more or less important than anyone else.

This is not what God intended. Jesus said, "You know that the rulers of the Gentiles lord it over them, and their high officials exercise authority over them. Not so with you. Instead, whoever wants to become great among you must be your servant, and whoever wants to be first must be your slave — just as the Son of Man did not come to be served, but to serve, and to give his life as a ransom for many."[14] We are not to accept for ourselves titles of honor, such as "father," or "teacher."[15]

Bruised egos are often the largest problem in resolving conflicts. Typically, one person feels slighted or hurt, and wants to "get even." Sometimes the purpose isn't so much to win as to cause the other person to lose. The "injured party" will not accept any solution that does not punish the other, even if it means being hurt himself.

A good place to start in conflict resolution is to express your sincere appreciation for the other person. If you are aware of past hurts, you could apologize and express sorrow for the hurt. When the other person feels you genuinely value and respect him or her, you can move on to other issues.

Seeking Mutual Interests

Clearly Paul was a person with an agenda. He got things done. He didn't passively give up on his purpose if he met resistance. He did not say we should give up on our own purposes, but that we should look *also* to the interests of others.

This principle is well illustrated by a model adapted from research literature.[16] Notice there are two main factors: **Assertiveness** has to do with how strongly I go after my own goals; **Cooperativeness** has to do with how strongly I help you go after your goals.

Here are the styles described:

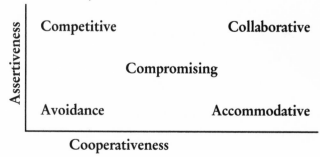

242

- Collaborative. This person is strong in both assertiveness and cooperativeness. The collaborative person will try to find a solution that fully meets his goals and also fully meets your goals. If such a solution can be found, both people win.

- Competitive. High in assertiveness, low in cooperativeness, this person wants her way, but doesn't care about you. This person may not feel she has "won" unless you have lost. This is a win-lose result. She may be very good at getting her way, but at the cost of the relationship.

- Accommodative. This person cares more about relationships than goals. At first accommodation seems like the Christian ideal, to sacrifice one's will for the will of others. However, if accommodation is taken to its extreme, the person would be totally at the mercy of others. He would have no agenda, no goal, no purpose, no witness. This person never says, "I won't do that" or "That's wrong." As Christians we have a God-given agenda! Excessive accommodation leads to a lose-win result.

- Avoidance. The person who is neither assertive nor cooperative just withdraws and does not deal with the conflict. He may be uninformed on the issue, it may not seem important to him, or he may be too lazy or frightened to get involved in the issue. Doing nothing usually results in both parties losing.

- Compromising. This is where I get some of what I want and you get some of what you want. It is not as good as collaborative, where we find a way to both get what we want. It is probably better than no solution at all.

Seek a collaborative solution so that both parties achieve their goals.

Bad Habits

One reason it's so difficult to resolve conflicts is that we have learned some bad habits that sabotage us. These include:

- Excessive competitiveness. We learn in school that competition is good and winning is better! In life, however, too much emphasis on competitiveness is counterproductive.

- Zero-sum assumption. In most sports there is only one winner, so if I win, you lose. My win and your loss add up to zero. This assumes we can't create any new "good"; we can only fight to divide what already exists. In life this is usually not true. People can create new resources, earn income, make a profit, see progress. We can often find ways to make it possible for both of us to win.

- Premature closure. We often jump to conclusions before we understand the issues or consider other possible solutions.

- Destructive redefinition. If it becomes my purpose to defeat you rather than find a mutually beneficial solution, we are both going to lose. Sometimes winning the argument becomes more important than solving the problem.[17]

- Pressure toward conformity. Cohesive groups tend to value conformity and stifle evaluation during decision making. They often make choices without adequate evaluation.

- Two-value thinking. We tend to reduce things to just two categories: good and bad, black and white, us and them. We forget the middle, the shades of gray. In two-value thinking we see people as either more similar to ourselves than they really are, or more different. Isn't it amazing how a dating couple will tend to see each other as very similar in almost every regard? But after they break up, they can see no similarity at all!

Avoidance and Escalation

Successful conflict resolution involves walking a tightrope between two extremes, avoidance on one side and escalation on the other.

A major reason for avoiding conflict is fear of losing or harming the relationship. David is dating Meg, an attractive and popular woman. He is bothered by her seeming lack of respect for him, the way she takes him for granted. He would like to discuss it with her, but is afraid to bring it up for fear of losing her. Meanwhile, Meg lowers her opinion of David because of his obvious fear of confronting her. She senses he is bothered about something. She wishes he would just "be a man" and talk to her about it.

About this time David gets acquainted with Joyce, a coworker at his office. Joyce is quiet and not as popular as Meg, but she is pretty and seems genuinely interested in him. Their friendship grows as they see each other around the office, and David perceives that Joyce would like to go out with him.

This changes the situation. Now David feels he has an alternative if he breaks up with Meg, so he is less fearful of losing the relationship. He almost doesn't care if Meg dumps him. He even considers breaking off with her.

One night when he is taking Meg home after a concert, he rather bluntly broaches the subject of her lack of respect for him. Meg is surprised, but after some initial bluster is relieved to get the issue out into the open. Eventually she apologizes for her insensitivity. David apologizes for not bringing it up sooner. Their relationship becomes stronger than ever.[18]

Avoidance leads to a downward spiral. You don't bring up the issue because you don't want to damage the relationship. Eventually the unresolved issues themselves damage the relationship. The

Face up to conflicts.
Avoidance only makes them worse.

weakened relationship becomes even more fragile until it finally self-destructs under the weight of the accumulated problems.

You can tell you are in an avoidance situation if people:[19]

- avoid bringing up controversial issues;

- spend too much time on trivial issues;

- don't seem to care about solving problems;

- don't want to consider difficult facts;

- are unusually quiet;

- adopt a "Why should we care?" attitude.

The opposite extreme is the upward spiral we call escalation. Ruth has been boiling for days and she finally blows up at her husband Jim, who is sitting in an easy chair reading a paper. She snatches the paper out of his hands. "You lazy son of a gun. If I let you, you would just sit there all day long and read that stupid paper."

Jim (surprised): "What's wrong with you? I always read the paper."

Ruth: "Yes, you do, and I always do all the work. You never lift a finger."

Jim: "And I suppose the eight hours I put in at work doesn't count? You just try it for a while and you'll see what it's like to be tired."

Ruth: "Oh, I know what it's like to be tired. You only work eight hours. I work twenty-four."

Jim: "Work? You call that work? You watch television all day. You don't even know what work is."

And on it goes, each exaggerated statement bringing a more extreme response. The original issues are soon lost in a flood of verbal aggression. Worse, they may have permanently damaged their relationship. In a few cases, the combatants eventually apologize for their extreme behavior and are none-the-worse for the experience.

Notice what happens during escalation:

- issues become exaggerated and extreme;

- tension and open hostility grows;

- threats are made, consequences exaggerated;

- voices are raised;

- eye contact becomes a glare, or is avoided;

- sarcastic remarks are made;

- names are called;

- the focus becomes more on personal aggression than on finding solutions.

A Balanced Approach

We have seen that neither avoidance of difficult issues nor too sharp an expression of anger is very productive. Paul calls for balance, " 'In your anger do not sin,' Do not let the sun go down while you are still angry."[20] It's not wrong to *feel* angry. We all feel anger when we are frustrated. We are made that way.

It's also OK to express anger. But Paul tells us not to express anger in a sinful way, and not to nurse anger for a long time. When we feel irritation, frustration and anger, we are in danger of sinning. We might do or say something to hurt another person.

The Proverbs have great wisdom about dealing with anger. Several verses make the point that we should be slow to anger.[21] I think that may refer to two factors, quantity and time. It should take quite a bit of aggravation to anger us. We can't afford to fly off the handle with every minor irritation. I'm talking to myself here. I sometimes get irritated if the waiter is a little tardy in bringing my soup. That's silly, counterproductive, and a waste of time and energy.

We also should take quite a bit of time before we express anger. I have sometimes become quite upset about a situation before I really understood it. And I'm not the only one. When the tribes east of the Jordan returned home after helping Israel capture their land, they built an altar to the Lord. When Phinehas, the priest, found out about it, he gave them a severe dressing down. Among other things he said, "How could you turn away from the LORD and build yourselves an altar in rebellion against him now?" Then they explained this wasn't an altar of rebellion but a symbol to help them remember the Lord. Oops. After they explained their purpose, Phinehas was pleased.[22]

Take time before expressing anger. Don't "boil over" too easily.

Proverbs also gives us some principles on how to deal with other people's anger. "A gentle answer turns away wrath, but a harsh word stirs up anger."[23] In a potential escalation situation, a gentle answer could avoid the whole thing. For example, after Ruth said, "You lazy son of a gun. If I let you, you would just sit there all day long and read that stupid paper," Jim could have said something like, "I'm sorry, I guess I have been ignoring you. What would you like me to do?"

Answer exaggerated charges softly so the situation does not escalate.

It's hard to respond to anger with gentleness. When we feel attacked, we want to respond in kind, or worse. But if we understand where that path leads, we will wisely want to choose another. The alternative is colorfully described in this Proverb: "For as churning the milk produces butter, and twisting the nose produces blood, so stirring up anger produces strife."[24] In a volatile situation I can either calm myself and give a gentle answer, or stir up my anger and give an answer that leads to escalation and strife.

We form response patterns, habits that are sometimes hard to break. Those who typically respond to situations in counterproductive ways are called fools in the Proverbs: "It is to a man's honor to avoid strife, but every fool is quick to quarrel."[25] "A fool gives full vent to his anger, but a wise man keeps himself under control."[26] "Do you see a man who speaks in haste? There is more hope for a fool than for him."[27] "A fool finds no pleasure in understanding but delights in airing his own opinions."[28]

So that we don't pick up their habits, we are warned not to associate with fools: "Do not make friends with a hot-tempered man, do not associate with one easily angered, or you may learn his ways and get yourself ensnared."[29] I saw this happen when a woman I know started dating a man with a fiery temper. In a very short time she became short-tempered too.

A Problem-solving Procedure

Staying away from the pitfalls of avoidance and escalation is a good way to begin resolving conflicts, but we need more to get us all the way to an excellent solution. The widely-used *Reflective Thinking Process*[30] is helpful here. The steps are as follows.

- Define the problem. What exactly is the problem? Is it even worth our effort and time? Get group members' opinions as to the nature and severity of the problem and try to work toward consensus on a definition. Sometimes solutions will be obvious once you agree on the nature of the problem.

- Analyze the problem and establish criteria for solution. What are the causes? How, when, and why did the problem start? What would a successful solution be like? What qualities would be necessary in a solution and which others would also be desirable?[31]

- Generate possible solutions. Develop as wide an array of possible solutions as you can. Reward creativity. Do not evaluate or eliminate solutions yet.

- Choose best solution. Now evaluate the possibilities and select the solution that best meets the group's (or individuals') goals. If no suitable solutions are found, go back to the step of searching for possible solutions. Don't give up too quickly.

- Carry out solution. Plan concrete steps to put the idea into effect. Assign responsibility.

Use a systematic problem-solving technique in which you define and analyze the problem, consider criteria for solution, generate possible solutions, choose the best one, and then implement it.

This method offers several benefits because it gives a logical order. We often waste time trying to solve a problem before we have a clear idea of what the problem is. We settle on less than an ideal solution because we don't take the time to creatively find a better one. Sometimes after we "solve" a problem nothing happens because we do not plan for any specific action.

To help us get through this procedure, Hall and Watson[32] suggest the following.

- Avoid arguing. Present your points clearly and seriously consider the reactions and opinions of others.

- Avoid "win-lose" statements. In an ideal solution no one loses.

- Don't change your mind just to avoid conflict, but be flexible when there is a reason to change your mind.

- Don't decide prematurely, just to avoid conflict. Voting before the issue has been fully discussed will likely result in a poor decision.

- Differences of opinion are helpful and lead to better decisions.

- View early agreement suspiciously. Make sure people are agreeing for good reasons.

Creating Better Solutions

Perhaps the prime difficulty in finding a win-win solution is lack of creativity. As mentioned earlier, if life is a "zero-sum game" in which there is only a limited amount of good, what I gain you lose. Then we focus on finding a fair way to divide the limited resources. Usually life isn't like that. There are other alternatives we can discover or create that make it possible for both of us to win.

Take time to find a better solution. Don't assume you must compromise too soon.

Finding the better solution is the problem. If the win-win solution were obvious, there would be no dispute. A married couple with small children has saved enough money to replace one of their older cars with a new one. She thinks they should buy a new station wagon because they need it for the family, and the old one is unreliable. He thinks they should buy a new sporty car for him to drive to work because he must drive farther and it would enhance his image at work.

Because there is only enough money to buy one new car (win-lose, zero-sum assumption) how do they resolve it? Many solutions might be possible, but one is that for the price of one new car they could buy two three-year-old cars, so both would get what they wanted. That solution is fairly obvious, but might not occur during the heat of an argument.

How do you become more creative in your thinking? Here are some suggestions.[33]

- Brainstorm to generate as many different solutions as possible. Keep on thinking of alternative solutions even after you have found one good possibility. There may be a better one! The more choices you have, the better your chance of finding a good solution.

- Don't assume there is only one right answer or acceptable solution.

- Separate the creation and evaluation functions. Premature judging will stifle creativity. When someone comes up with an idea, reward his or her creativity, don't shoot it down with reasons why it won't work.

- Remember that even obviously unworkable ideas are often valuable because they help us explore new territory and lead to ideas that can work.

- Break the rules. We often unconsciously follow "rules" dictated by custom or false assumptions. Breaking out of these unnecessary constraints frees us to see new possibilities.

- Be playful. Creativity often runs counter to logic. Dare to think of solutions that seem impossible.

- Key off each other. Another person may come up with a far out idea, which makes you think of another, and so on.

- Play "what if?" What if money were no object? What if we lived in another part of the country? What if I changed jobs? etc., etc.

- Don't be too afraid of making mistakes. Errors are often a necessary part of finding a better solution. Too much caution leads to fear of innovation which results in missing the best solutions.

Creating a Climate for Conflict Resolution

Different groups, churches, couples, families, etc., have different cultures or "climates" in which the members interact with each other. The climates are group norms or habits of interaction. They tend to be relatively stable, but can be changed.

Create a climate of trust, openness, and fairness which make conflict resolution easier.

Here are some factors that contribute to a climate favorable to conflict resolution.

- Members trust each other and feel safe;
- members know each other well and talk deeply with each other;
- the group is open to new ideas;
- the group is fair;
- there is a sense of group identity;
- members value and are committed to the group;
- members depend on each other. All gain if the group succeeds and lose if the group fails; and
- members can express their feelings to each other.

Chapter Summary

Conflicts often spring from greed. They are difficult to solve because we feel our rights are being denied. A true humility is possible when we realize our worth to God. We must also realize that we are no more important than others.

Using a collaborative style in problem solving, I seek to fulfill my own goals at the same time I try to help you fulfill yours. That's a win-win approach. We often assume a compromise or a "I win; you lose" situation is the best available, but greater persistence and creativity can often find a genuine "win-win" solution.

Avoidance and escalation are two extremes to avoid. In avoidance neither party brings the problem up until the weight of the problem ruins the relationship. The opposite is escalation, where each party exaggerates the problem in an upward spiral of temper, accusations, and bad feelings. Both approaches are counterproductive.

While Scripture does not condemn anger it does have a great deal to say about how to express it. We should be slow to anger and answer gently. A rational problem-solving technique begins with defining the problem, establishing criteria for a solution, generating possible solutions, choosing the best solution, and carrying it out. A crucial part is to take the time to find a solution that lets both parties achieve their goals.

1. See James 1:2.
2. See James 4:1-3.
3. See 2 Samuel 12:7-10.
4. See, for example, Matthew 7:7; Philippians 4:19.
5. See Romans 8:32.
6. See Philippians 4:12-13.
7. See Philippians 2:1-11.
8. See 1 Corinthians 6:1-8.
9. See Luke 6:27-31.
10. See Matthew 21:12.
11. See Luke 22:36.
12. See Philippians 2:3-4.
13. See Romans 12:3.
14. See Matthew 20:25-38.
15. See Matthew 23:8-11.
16. R.R. Blake and J.S. Mounton, *The Management Grid* (Houston: Gulf Publishing, 1964).
17. This, and several points that follow, are adapted from Joseph P. Folger

and Marshall Poole, *Working through Conflict* (Glenview, Ill.: Scott, Foresman and Company, 1984).

18. This fictional story illustrates research findings discussed by Michael Roloff and Denise Cloven, "The Chilling Effect in Interpersonal Relationships: The Reluctance to Speak One's Mind," in *Intimates in Conflict: A Communication Perspective*, ed. Dudley Cahn (Hillsdale, NJ: Lawrence Erlbaum Associates, 1990) 49–75.

19. Adapted from Folger and Poole, *Working through Conflict*, 78.

20. Ephesians 4:26.

21. See Proverbs 14:29; 15:18; 16:32; 19:11.

22. See Joshua 22:10-31.

23. See Proverbs 15:1.

24. See Proverbs 30:33.

25. See Proverbs 20:3.

26. See Proverbs 29:11.

27. See Proverbs 29:20.

28. See Proverbs 18:2.

29. See Proverbs 22:24-25.

30. Scheidel, T., and Crowell, L., *Discussing and Deciding* (New York: Macmillan, 1979). This procedure is applied to conflict resolution in Folger and Poole, *Working through Conflict*.

31. Dividing the solution characteristics into "musts" and "wants" is recommended by C. Kepner and B. Tregoe, *The Rational Manager: A Systematic Approach to Problem Solving and Decision Making* (New York: McGraw-Hill, 1985).

32. J. Hall and W.H. Watson, "The Effects of a Normative Intervention on Group Decision-making Performance," *Human Relations* 23 (1970): 299–317.

33. Some of these are adapted from a very innovative book: Roger von Oech, *A Whack on the Side of the Head: How to Unlock Your Mind for Innovation* (New York: Warner Books, 1983).

Enhance Memory and
Promote Change

CHAPTER SIXTEEN

Help Your Audience Remember

To get people to do something, first you must capture and hold their attention, and then provide a message they understand. They must also remember the message until they have a chance to act on it.

How much of a message do people remember? One researcher had several experienced college teachers prepare 10-minute talks in their fields of expertise. Students listening to each talk knew they would be tested, but they could only remember 50 percent of the points immediately after the lecture. Two weeks later they could only remember 25 percent.[1]

Realize most of what you say will soon be forgotten.

If these motivated college students could only remember half the points from a 10-minute talk when tested immediately afterward, how much of a typical sermon or class do people remember?

Immediate, Short-term, and Long-term Memory

Researchers use different words to describe the categories of memory.[2] I have chosen to call them immediate, short-term, and long-term. Immediate memory lasts for about 15 seconds. You can renew it by recalling the information into consciousness, as you do when trying to remember a phone number between looking it up and dialing. By repeatedly bringing up the number into consciousness every few seconds, you can remember it indefinitely.

Of course, something often happens to distract you for a few seconds, then you lose it. Many times I have become distracted between the phone book and the phone and had to look up a number again.

Through immediate memory we can remember almost anything for about 15 seconds. After that the vast majority of information fades from our consciousness with little hope of retrieval.

Short-term memory lasts just a few minutes. It serves as the gateway to long-term memory. Unless we first become conscious of something, we will not remember it. We will be more likely to remember something if we rehearse it or think about it, rather than just letting it slide into oblivion.

If we want to remember something longer, we must either rehearse it many times in short-term memory or associate it with something we already have stored in long-term memory.

For example, if you want to remember a verse, you first read it, then repeat it several times. Eventually, it transfers into long-term memory. But, as we know all too well, we must refresh the memory with periodic rehearsal.

Most people do not rehearse information enough so that it is firmly fixed in long-term memory. If you practice only until you can say a passage of Scripture without error, you will not remember it long. The reason is that you are using a mixture of short-term and long-term memory. The short-term portion will fade away soon after you stop rehearsing it, and the verse will be forgotten.

Overlearning will help to cement information into long-term memory. Overlearning means continuing to rehearse even after you can successfully repeat a passage. One hundred percent overlearning is often recommended. That is, if it takes five minutes to get to the point where you can repeat a passage without error, continue to rehearse it another five minutes.

Long-term memory is well-organized. A function of short-term memory is to organize incoming material and help it fit into categories already established in long-term memory. If the material presented is poorly organized, more work must be done in short-term memory to sort it out and make it fit. While this is happening, some new information coming in will be lost. That's why well-organized information is remembered better.

Verbal Memory Aids

Here are some tips to help you present information in a way that will be easy to remember.

- Organize the material well.

- Use an "advance organizer," a brief statement that tells audience members how the material is organized. This is useful unless the method of organization is obvious.

- Help the audience sort out the material and identify the most important points. Sometimes speakers say something like, "If you only remember one thing from this message, remember this."

- Repeat the important points several times. Even get the audience to repeat them or write them down. Tony Campolo has a wonderful sermon in which he gets the entire congregation to repeat the theme many times, "It's Friday, but Sunday's coming." You can't help but remember the point of that message!

261

- Things from the beginning and end of the message will be remembered best. Use these times to make or emphasize your best points.

- Meaningful information is remembered better than ideas that are not understood. Don't do what we professors often do — present new ideas by using unfamiliar words.

- Use an analogy to relate the new idea to something people are already familiar with. Help them to see how the new idea is the same as or different from what they already know. Much of Jesus' teaching used analogies to very familiar aspects of life, such as planting and harvest.

- Illustrate your ideas using a story. Stories are easier to remember than abstract principles.

- Review the material. You can summarize points made earlier in the same message, and review points from previous messages in later messages.

Telling Stories

Jesus sometimes preached sermons, but his most characteristic method of teaching was telling stories. The stories were about people and situations the audience could understand easily. Each story made a profound spiritual point.

Because people can't see or handle spiritual things, such things seem hard to understand. We can make the spiritual easier to understand by relating it to well-known physical things.

Tell stories.

In Luke 15 Jesus tells three stories: the Parables of the Lost Sheep, Lost Coin, and Lost Son. They all make the same point. My friend Dr. Don Miller, was a missionary to Africa. He

262

noticed Jesus' method was the same as a traditional African teaching style. He tried using a series of stories and found it worked better than the traditional western style of logical argument. Here are some storytelling tips.

- The story should be relevant to the point you are trying to make. In high school we found we could keep our history teacher off the topic by asking him to tell war stories. We enjoyed the stories but learned very little history.

- Tell stories about people. If you want to tell about an organization, for example, frame it in terms of the people involved. People enjoy stories about other people.

- Use curiosity and surprise. Your story should give some hint that it contains a surprise element. If it seems predictable, people will lose interest. Arrange the elements of the story so you don't give away the surprise too soon.

- Let your audience identify with someone in the story. If people can see themselves in the story, it will be more powerful.

- Use enough facts so the story seems real, but don't get bogged down in unnecessary detail. I once had a coworker who seemed to be unable to tell even the simplest story in less than 15 minutes.

- Include emotions. Tell how the person felt. Depict the silly grin or the tears leaking out.

- Make it visual. Describe some of the details. Help people form colorful images in their minds.

- Get excitement into your voice as you tell your story. Be enthusiastic, even dramatic.

Visual Memory Aids

The grade school idea of "show and tell" is a good one because it gives us both the strength of visual images plus words. I have noticed, for example, that just telling students how to load a camera is not nearly as effective as both showing and telling.

Show and tell.
Both demonstrate and describe an action
you want people to learn.

Communicators should use both visual images and words together whenever possible. Field trips and demonstrations can be powerful learning tools. You can use film or video to effectively help learners visualize. You can describe visual images which the listeners create in their minds. You can also help listeners mentally rehearse an action by asking them to visualize the steps as they say them aloud.

Drama

I don't envy the prophets. They not only had an unpopular message, but they often had to use methods that were decidedly inconvenient. Take Ezekiel. He had to lie on his left side for 390 days, symbolizing the 390 years of rebellion of Israel. He ate only a special bread, baked over cow manure, and drank water while lying on his left side for more than a year.

What was God's purpose in having His servants do such bizarre things? It seems to me God needed something with more impact than just words. Such unusual activities would capture the imagination and curiosity. They make their points in different ways than words do.

A dramatic presentation in church affects people in a different and often a more substantial way than a sermon. It's more visual. It impacts more of the senses.

It was Easter and the church was packed. The pastor had just launched into his message on "Evidences for the Resurrection."

Suddenly, a man we didn't recognize stood up and shouted out, "I've sat here as long as I can listening to this rubbish. I can't believe you are still teaching that old Resurrection myth." The pastor seemed shocked. After sputtering a bit, he asked the man what it was he objected to. The stranger replied there was no evidence Jesus ever lived, let alone that he had been raised from the dead. A dialogue developed as the pastor answered his objections, only to have him raise more.

The dialogue continued for several minutes, objections followed by answers. Finally, the pastor let us in on the ruse. The man was a professional actor from a neaby town. The whole thing was staged and both played their parts so well almost no one suspected. It was that real. And it was memorable. Over 20 years later it is still fresh in my mind.

Drama can be used in a variety of ways. Often a short drama can be used to introduce the topic for a message. You could weave a mini drama throughout a sermon. The action could freeze or the lights black out while the speaker discusses the significance of what is happening. At other times a drama could be the entire message. You could follow the drama with discussion. It is the nature of drama that it often leaves unanswered questions. These can inspire a fruitful discussion period. (See Appendix A for an example of a short drama about the nature of God.)

Film and Video

Film and video are powerful means for telling stories. They are extensions of the traditional oral methods used by Jesus and many others. There are many strong Christian films available through film distributors. The latest are usually in film format, suitable for showing to a congregation or class. After a year or two, they are then released on video. Many Christian bookstores now carry a wide range of videos.

You could also create your own videos. Lend a youth group a camcorder and give them a principle to illustrate. Allow about 20 minutes to figure out how to act out the scenario and tape it, then have everyone watch it and discuss it afterward. Topics could include: what to do if someone wants you to do something you know is wrong (drugs, sex, drinking); what to say when someone asks you why you don't drink or do drugs; what to say to someone who doesn't believe in God.

Use Christian films and videos in your home, Sunday School, and church.

Create Monuments

In several cases when the Lord did a remarkable thing, the Israelites set up a monument to help them remember it. Jacob built a pillar on the rock where he dreamed of the ladder to heaven.[3] The Israelites built a pillar where God divided the Jordan River.[4] A monument is a relatively permanent physical object that reminds you of something important. Here are some ways you can make monuments of important events in your spiritual life.

Create physical things that you will see to remind you of spiritual milestones.

- Hang something on the wall. My wife and I have a beautiful, hand-embroidered sampler commemorating our wedding day. It reminds me of how blessed I am to have such a wife, and that I made some sacred vows on that day.

- Frame your certificates. Do you have a baptismal certificate? Hang it.

- Visit significant locations. I accepted the Lord and made other important decisions in camps near Mt. Hood, Oregon. Even just seeing the mountain is special to me because it reminds me of these events.

Use Written Reminders

God told the Israelites to set up large stones and write the words of the law on them.[5] They also wrote the law on the door posts of their homes.[6] We too can surround ourselves with written reminders about godly living.

- Encourage children to write words or make pictures that remind them of Bible stories or principles, then post these around the house.

- Type Scripture verses on 3 x 5 cards and carry them in your car. Glance at them when stopped at lights, etc.

- A verse on the bathroom mirror will get noticed every morning.

- A Bible on the coffee table is an invitation to read.

> **Surround yourself with signs, cards, and other reminders of spiritual truths you want to remember.**

- A pastor or teacher could regularly have small cards printed with reference verses and key thoughts from messages. A different card could be passed out for each session, keyed to that day's lesson. Over time, attenders would build a deck of these cards which they could use for review and memorization.

- Create banners or posters for your teaching/worship
  space. These could vary from simple bulletin board displays to elaborate hand-sewn banners. Maybe there is a
  spiritual "Betsy Ross" in your group.

Incorporating Learning Styles

People who write and read books are probably highly verbal, so
we tend to forget that not everyone learns most easily from
words. Take learning to drive. Some can learn by just reading
about it. Others have a hard time understanding until they see
pictures or diagrams. Some don't really get the idea until they
sit in the driver's seat and get the tactile feel of the experience.

There are many ways to think about learning styles.[7] One of
the best known is a formulation by David Kolb which he calls,
"Experiential Learning."[8] In his model he pictures learning as a
circle which starts with "concrete experience," actually doing
something. This is followed by "reflective observation," that is,
thinking about the experience. Next comes "abstract conceptualization," trying to come up with general principles suggested
by the experience. The last step is "active experimentation" in
which the new principles are tried out. Then the circle repeats.

For example, if I wanted to teach students to operate a video
camera, I could first give them the camera and let them shoot
some tape. Then we would take a look at the tape and think
about what it looked like. From our experiences and thoughts
we would try to come up with some principles of videography,
which we would then try out. Finally, we would be ready to
start the whole process all over, but this time the tapes should
be considerably better.

Suppose you want to prepare people to be good Sunday
School teachers. Using Kolb's model, you would let them teach
a lesson or a part of a lesson, then think about the experience,
try to come up with some principles for better teaching, try
these out, then repeat the entire process.

Kolb points out that some people prefer one style and others
prefer another, but by using all four modes everyone under-

stands. One researcher found that retention improved from 20 percent using abstract conceptualization alone (a traditional lecture) to 90 percent when a professor used all four modes.[9] Here are some other differences in learning styles.

- Some people like to analyze something before attempting it, others (like me) are more impulsive and just want to jump in and try it.

- Some like to dissect an idea and analyze the details, others prefer to take a broader view.

- Some prefer to work alone, others like to work in groups.

- Some people think deeply and learn by analysis, others learn mostly by memorization.

- Some prefer concrete, hands-on experience. Others prefer theory.

Two approaches are possible in trying to find the message style that most suits your audience. The first would require you to find out what styles your audience prefers. With most audiences I believe you would find quite a range of style preferences although most people do not prefer the "abstract conceptualization" style most used by teachers!

Use different teaching methods to appeal to people with different learning styles.

Another approach is simply to try different styles. By doing this, you will hit everyone's preference at least some of the time. You will also get some flack from those who prefer the traditional lecture style. Gradually, you will learn what works and what doesn't work for your particular audience.

Active Learning

While there is a place for listening to lectures, reading books, and quiet reflection, many of us learn best when we are more active. I vividly remember when I went through a program to learn how to tell others about my faith. I especially remember the part where I actually went out and did it!

Have learners engage in physical activities as part of learning.

A secular text in persuasion[10] attributes some of Billy Graham's effectiveness to the fact that he does not just ask people to make a decision. He asks them very specifically to rise from their seats and walk to the front of the auditorium.

In active learning we are not just learning from the situation around us, we are also learning from the fact that we are doing something. A person going forward in a crusade has her momentary decision to begin the trip confirmed as she senses that she is going forward. I received Christ at the age of 10 at a camp. I still vividly remember the sensation of handing the chorus book to another boy, leaving my seat, and walking forward. To a timid boy that was a real step of faith. It was also a confirmation to myself that I had made a decision.

Active learning also has the benefit of stimulating a higher degree of alertness, at least for many of us. One could go to sleep while studying about acting, but it's hard to sleep while doing it. (It did happen once during a college production I was attending. An actor, who was playing a hospitalized patient, drifted off to sleep and even snored during the performance. Another actor awakened him, and most of the audience thought it was part of the script!)

Here are some ideas for making learning more active.

- Visit locations. Take the class or congregation to locations such as rescue missions, inner city ministries, museums, colleges, etc. Go to a camp, the seashore, the mountains, etc. Just getting to a different location often helps us strip away the ordinary and see things differently.

- Use role-playing. Assign roles to members. Acting ability is not very important. Give them a simple situation, and let them ad-lib lines. This can be a great way to get into a topic or illustrate a problem. Then you can discuss the problem and later have class members role-play a solution. You could also break the class into smaller teams and have each team come up with a role-play for a possible solution. A role-play might take two to five minutes.

- Use simulations. Similar to a role-play, but the roles and situation are more highly defined with the aim of making it as lifelike as possible. A simulation might take 15 to 30 minutes.

- Use discussion. The teacher could set up a situation, raise some pertinent questions, then ask for discussion. Discussion is best when there is more than one "correct" answer. It's very frustrating to the class if the teacher tries to funnel the discussion to a particular solution. For example, it would be difficult to have a discussion on the question: "Is the earth round?"

- Incorporate more testimonials into group activities. If your group has trouble getting started, ask one or two people in advance to be ready to share. Once someone has started, others will usually follow. Testimonials can be on many topics, including how a person became a Christian, answers to prayers, difficult situations they have come through, and especially struggles they are currently undergoing.

- Give participants a problem to solve or a question to answer. The question could be on a handout or projected on

271

a screen. Have them break into groups of two or three and discuss it for two minutes. You could then let representatives of some of the groups report their findings to the large group.

- Involve all family members in family worship. Use them in ways they are gifted and are appropriate for their age. Be prepared to sacrifice some elegance for increased vitality and authenticity.

Culturally Relevant Messages

When Paul spoke in Athens, he noticed the people were very religious. Among their many altars was one to an unknown God.[11] Paul uses this observation as a beginning point to relate the truth. He did not refer to the Hebrew Scriptures, which would have been unknown and irrelevant to the Greeks in Athens.

On the other hand, when Peter spoke on the day of Pentecost to a Jewish crowd, he cited Scripture several times.[12] The people were experiencing something new. How could they know if it was from God? Peter, knowing his audience, cited Scripture right away.

When Paul mentioned becoming "all things to all men"[13] he meant we should be sensitive to the situation of the hearer and adapt the message accordingly. Some people resist this. They somehow equate a change in the presentation style with a compromise in the content.

When I was teaching at a secular university in Connecticut, I was privileged to help a student who was a baby Christian take his first faltering steps of faith. He had been saved from a life of drugs. A rock drummer, he was one of the wildest looking students I ever met. As a new Christian, he devoured the Word and grew rapidly. I had the opportunity to steer him toward a summer internship at Campus Crusade in California. While there he discovered contemporary Christian music.

What a revolution that was in his life. He absolutely loved it, not only for the rock beat but especially for the spiritual words. He took nonbelievers for rides in his car so he could play the music for them. Up to that point I was hardly aware there was such a thing as contemporary Christian music. When I saw how it blessed and ministered to this young Christian, and how he used it in witnessing, I realized its value.

The point of all this is that we should adapt our message style to fit the communication style, culture, and background of the receiver.

Using Mnemonic Aids

Mnemonics are mental tricks or strategies we can use to help us remember better. Some have been in use since ancient times. The basic idea is to memorize a sequence of things to serve as a framework. Then you create a vivid mental image joining something you are trying to remember with the framework you memorized earlier.

A common device is to memorize a rhyming word for each number through ten. One my grandmother taught me years ago is: 1: bun; 2: shoe; 3: tree; 4: door; 5: hive; 6: sticks; 7: heaven; 8: gate; 9: line; 10: hen. Let's say I need to bring home several things from the office: my briefcase, a check, a letter, and a book. I could visualize it this way: I could see my briefcase in the middle of a giant hamburger bun. I could visualize a check written on the tongue of a shoe. There could be a tree with letters for leaves, and finally a giant book being used as a door. The more vivid and unusual the images I create the better I remember them. When I want to remember the sequence, I just start with my previously memorized: 1: Bun, and see the picture of my briefcase in the bun . . . and so on.[14]

Here are some other common mnemonic devices you might try.

- Location. Think of a place you are quite familiar with, then mentally walk through it, associating a point you wish to remember with something at that location. For example if I stand in our kitchen, I have the sink to my left, a counter with a phone straight ahead, a television set a little to the right, a stove hard to my right, and a breadmaking machine behind me. I create vivid mental images linking the points in a speech I am making to each of these locations. Then I can remember them just by mentally strolling around my kitchen. For more points I could mentally walk into other rooms.

■ Initial letters. The common trick of forming a word out of the first letters of several words you wish to remember is a good one. For example, the word *Aida* (which happens to be the name of an opera) stands for four steps in writing radio commercials: Attention, Interest, Desire, Action. It helps if the word makes sense, and it would be best if it were related to the topic.

■ A variation on initial letters is to create a new sentence using them. Anyone who has studied music knows that the lines of the treble clef, e, g, b, d, f, are remembered by "Every good boy does fine." The spaces of the treble clef spell out "face."

■ A chain. If you have several things to remember, create a single image that includes all of the points. For example, if I need to remember to phone a colleague, have my car serviced, and prepare a quiz, I could imagine my colleague servicing my car and wiping the dip stick on my newly prepared quiz.

■ Create a sentence. Sometimes words can be added to the words you wish to remember to create a sentence that makes sense (although it can be fanciful). The numbers one through five in Japanese are: ichi, ni, san, shi, go. I learned to remember them by thinking of a Japanese woman named Ichi Ni. Because the Japanese add the honorary term "san" at the end of names, Ichi Ni would be addressed as Ichi Ni San. Then it's easy to imagine a person in broken English telling me, "Ichi Ni San, she go."

In preparing material for others you probably can discover ways to help them remember the information better. You could use the method of location, for example. You would create a description of visual images they could create at various points in the room where you are meeting. Initial letters that make up a word might be hard to create, but would be easy to remember.

Create easy-to-remember sentences or words to help your audience remember important information.

Alliteration (using the same first letter) has long been used for helping people remember the points of an outline. However, it often requires the speaker to use an unfamiliar or arcane word to represent the point.

Deciding What to Remember

It's said there was once a time when a well-educated person could know most of what was known. Now is not that time. Growth in population, travel, technology, science, and means of communication has conspired to inundate us with a flood of information beyond our ability to process. Extensive indexing systems help us get to the particular passage we need. Home computers can now go "on line" with huge databases at low cost. CD-ROM and large, inexpensive hard drives make it feasible for many to have almost instant access to a huge array of information stored in their own systems. The trend, then, is helping people easily find the information they need when they need it, instead of trying to remember it all.

As a message sender, here are some fundamental questions you need to ask yourself.

- How much, if any, of this information does my audience need to remember (that is, to store in their brains)? Could they more easily find the information when needed?

- How can I help them remember the parts they need to remember?

- How much are they likely to remember? As important as the information may be, and as much as you would like them to remember it, is that a reasonable expectation?

- If they are unlikely to remember the information, will they be able to find it when they need it?

- How can I package the information so they can find it when they need it?

The kind of information people need to store in the mind rather than on paper or computer includes important facts needed on very short notice when there would not be time or opportunity to look it up. This includes information about health and safety and things related to purpose and direction.

Don't expect your audience to remember everything. Help them separate out the few things they need to remember, and know how they can find the other information when they need it.

Reminding People to Remember

This chapter has already dealt with ideas to help people remember. Here are some ideas to help people get back to information they are almost certainly going to forget.

- Encourage them to take notes. An effective way of doing this is to prepare some structured notes. You put in the main categories and leave blank space or blanks in the lines for them to fill in. The act of filling the blank will help them remember the item, and the sheet becomes something they can refer to later.

- At times note-taking can interfere with listening. Instead, ask people to just listen for five minutes or so. Then pause for a minute or two to let them take notes while you are not talking. (Of course the idea of not talking for a couple of minutes horrifies some of us!)

- Hand out a detailed syllabus, outline, or notes. For most of my classes I prepare a detailed outline of all the main points, giving space to write in details. I sometimes include questions to answer or blanks to fill in. For a course the syllabus is usually bound. For individual sessions, such as Sunday School lessons, I like to make a detailed handout. It's a good idea to three-hole-punch it, and point out that it is part of a series. Then it is more likely to be kept.

- Give audience members references so they can do additional research if and when they choose. This would include biblical references and books and other materials on the subject.

- Consider packaging a series of audiotapes or videotapes on a topic with a good outline to help listeners find the particular part of the series of most concern to them.

- Consider beginning a course or a series of messages by passing out folders or inexpensive three-ring binders. Have the notebooks printed with the name of the series on the front and the spine. (You could give away the notebooks or sell them at cost.) On the first day the notebook would include a table of contents for the entire series and a detailed outline of the first message. The table of contents could be modified later, if necessary. This method encourages people to take good notes and to keep them. It would also provide incentive to attend the entire series. Best of all, listeners would have an excellent way to go back to the material when needed.

Chapter Summary

People forget very quickly. If people are to retain information over time, they must make great effort. It is not enough to rehearse something until it can be repeated from memory. Considerably more practice is needed to embed something in long-term memory.

You can make things easier to remember by organizing them well and building in memory aids. Audience members will remember information better if they understand it well, and if they can associate it with things they already know. It is also important to review the material from time to time.

People tend to remember better if they are both told and shown, and different people learn most easily by different methods. Some are highly verbal, others learn best from observation, still others by physically doing things. You will enhance general learning if you use a mix of styles.

Unusual and unexpected things make a stronger impression and are remembered longer. Incorporate surprises into your presentations.

Remembering is hard work. Most people will quickly forget information. You can help your audience recognize the few things they need to memorize and those they can get back to when they need them. Also, you can encourage good note-taking by using structured notes or outlines. Giving references also helps people find information when they need it.

1. Ralph Nichols, "Do We Know How to Listen?" in *Communication Concepts and Process*, ed. Joseph DeVito (Englewood Cliffs, NJ: Prentice Hall, 1976).

2. A very readable review of the literature on memory is contained in Robert M.W. Travers, *Essentials of Learning*, 5th ed. (New York: Macmillan, 1982).

3. See Genesis 28:18.

4. See Joshua 4:3.

5. See Deuteronomy 27:2-3.

6. See Deuteronomy 6:9.

7. A concise and helpful summation of several learning styles is found in Charles Claxton and Patricia Murrell, *Learning Styles: Implications for Improving Educational Practices* (College Station, TX: Association for the Study of Higher Education, 1987).

8. David Kolb, *Experiential Learning: Experience as the Source of Learning and Development* (New York: Prentice Hall, 1984).

9. James E. Stice, "Using Kolb's Learning Cycle to Improve Student Learning," *Engineering Education* (February, 1987): 921–96.

10. Erwin P. Bettinghaus, *Persuasive Communication*, 3rd ed. (New York: Holt, Rinehart, and Winston, 1980).

11. See Acts 17:16-34.

12. See Acts 2:14ff.

13. See 1 Corinthians 9:22.

14. An excellent discussion of mnemonic processes, how and why they work from a theoretical viewpoint is found in Mark McDaniel and Michael Pressley, eds., *Imagery and Related Mnemonic Processes: Theories, Individual Differences and Applications* (New York: Springer-Verlag, 1987). A breezy "how to" book on mnemonic devices is William D. Hersey, *Blueprints for Memory: Your Guide to Remembering Business Facts, Figures & Faces* (Saranac Lake, NY: AMACOM, 1991).

CHAPTER SEVENTEEN

Promote Action

T he road to hell is paved with good intentions."

It's well known in psychology literature that attitudes and intentions do not necessarily lead to actions.[1] I also know this from personal experience. For several years I intended to lose weight. But the intention, sincere as it was, never produced any weight loss. Until I actually made a commitment and began a diet, I made no progress.

Paul captured well the struggle with intentions: "For I have the desire to do what is good, but I cannot carry it out. For what I do is not the good I want to do; no, the evil I do not want to do—this I keep on doing."[2] We must recognize that as Christians we are no longer under bondage or obligation to our old evil nature, but we are free to follow the Spirit. We must *choose* to "put to death the misdeeds of the body."[3] Even though we have the Spirit of God to empower and guide us, we still must *choose* and *act!*

The purpose for studying the Bible is not just to know it, but to *do* it. In the book of James we read that we should not just be hearers of the Word, but doers. We are not blessed by just hearing, but by remembering and doing what we hear.⁴ Hearing alone leads to deception.

Why don't actions always follow intentions?

■ Intentions may be quickly forgotten. While driving, I hear of a book I would like to have and decide to call the number given and order the book as soon as I get home. But before I get home my mind is distracted by 1,000 other thoughts, and I forget my intention.

■ Intentions may be unrealistic. I sometimes have students who say their goal is to be a network news anchor. Why not? It's a highly paid, glamorous job. But the students are often unrealistic about what it takes to get to such an exalted position.

■ Social realities may hinder intentions. Often we need the approval or support of others. A person wants to complete his/her education, but finds the spouse is not willing to make the sacrifices necessary.

■ A person may not know how to accomplish the intention. Responding to a stirring sermon on loving your neighbor, a high school student wants to express love to his fellow students. How does he do it? Does he tell his friends he loves them? Does he give them hugs? These seem awkward, and he can't think of any more acceptable way to show love, so he does nothing.

■ Action may be procrastinated. Putting off the action to a later time may be a way to avoid the action altogether despite a sincere desire to follow through on the action. But the intention diminishes with time.

Communicating for Action

While we can't force people to act, we can clearly communicate in a way that will make most people more likely to act. Here are some ideas:

Ask

In sales it is well known that you must ask for the order. The other person will not usually take the initiative to ask what to do. You will be more effective if you suggest a course of action.

We are sometimes reluctant to ask because of fear of rejection. A man may not ask a woman he is attracted to for a date because he feels he could not bear the hurt and embarrassment if she said no. But, if he doesn't take the initiative, there is almost no chance they will get together. Sometimes people who would like to take a particular action do not do so because no one asks. Part of being an effective communicator is being willing to take the risk and ask for action.

When asking, however, you need to be sensitive to the position of the other person and not ask too much. Research shows the more you ask for the more you get, up to a certain point. Beyond that point the person may reject your request and devalue her relationship with you.[5]

Where is that point? Unfortunately, it's hard to tell. It depends, in part, on how much the individual values her relationship with you, and how strongly she feels about the issue. If you know the person well, you can ask for a fairly large change, particularly if you know she doesn't feel strongly about the issue. If you have just met the person, you will be safer if you ask for only a modest change in behavior.

Ask for Specific Action

Sometimes it is not clear what concrete actions would be appropriate. The Bible often links profound principles with particular actions. In the Book of Ephesians, for example, the first three chapters raise us to lofty theological heights, while the last three chapters are very "down to earth." They tell us very specifically what to do.

I believe one of the reasons people respond in such large numbers when Billy Graham gives an invitation is that he is very specific about what they should do. He says something like, "I want you to get up out of your seat and walk down here onto the playing field. If you came with others, they will wait." Then he tells them specifically what will happen when they get there.

Ask for Action Now

Because the intention to act and information about how to act will be quickly forgotten, communication will be most effective if you give people the opportunity to act immediately. If it is not possible to complete the action immediately, have them take a first step. For example, if you want your Sunday school class to give blood, it would be best to have the bloodmobile waiting outside. Next best would be to have them sign up immediately after you explain the need.

Have Your Receivers Make a Commitment

They should commit to a particular action within a specific time period. End a planning meeting by giving specific assignments to each individual. Get a verbal commitment to complete the work by a specific date. You could ask, "Alice, will you call these 10 people by next Tuesday?"

Ask people to make a commitment to a specific action to be completed by a particular time.

Compliance will be higher if you tell people you will be checking. You could say, "I'll call each of you on Monday to check on your progress." It's also effective to send a note or a copy of the minutes which details each person's commitment.

In a larger group situation, getting a commitment is more difficult, but still possible. You could ask people to write their commitment down on a card, along with their address. You could say you will return the card to them after a certain time period (say six weeks) as a reminder of their commitment.

You could have them make a promise to their spouse, or a friend. Suggest that this person hold them accountable and check with them periodically to find out how they are doing on their commitment. Or you could simply have them write out their commitment on a card and take it with them as a reminder.

Use Self-persuasion

While attitudes sometimes lead to actions, it's also true that actions lead to attitudes. If you can get a person to take even a small step in the direction you want him to go, two things will happen. If that small step was rewarding, he will want to repeat it. Also, knowing he has taken a step in a particular direction will probably change his attitude about the course of behavior.

For example, let's say you have a friend who has been vocally opposed to Christianity. You invite him to your home to meet some of your friends, and he has a great time. He becomes aware that most of your friends are Christians. He now realizes at least some Christians are OK.

Next you invite him to a social event at your church. He is aware that he, who hates Christianity, is actually at a church, and he's having a good time. He is beginning to persuade himself that maybe his assessment of Christianity (or at least of this church) was wrong. Next he might be willing to attend a Sunday School class or worship service.

If you ask him what he thought of the experience, you will give him another chance to persuade himself. If he says he enjoyed it, he will be aware he said it, and he will be more likely to believe it!

Urge people to take a small first step in the direction you want them to go.

The basic principle above is that there is internal pressure to maintain consistency between one's beliefs and actions. If a person acts in a way incompatible with his beliefs, he will feel pressure to change his beliefs because the action is hard to deny.

Make It Easy to Act

It's a wonder some radio commercials get any response at all. The announcer rattles off a phone number or two and a street address. The poor listener gets confused with all the numbers and wouldn't be able to respond if she wanted to. If a store wants people to phone, they should get an easy-to-remember number. Instead of giving a street address with hard-to-remember numbers, the store could give its location in relation to some well-known landmark, such as, "We're on Imperial, just one block west of the Brea Mall. Look for our bright-green sign."

Make it clear what you want people to do and easy for them to do so.

Fundraisers know they will get a much larger response if they supply a "response device" and a preaddressed envelope along with an appeal letter. The potential donor may feel it's too much trouble to address an envelope and write a letter to enclose with a check. It's much easier just to check off the appropriate category and slip the check and response card into the preaddressed and stamped envelope.

Make It Non-threatening to Act

Sometimes an action has hidden negative repercussions. A friend of mine once gave a sizeable donation to a Christian organization. From that point on they hounded her for more, phoned, and even sent registered letters she had to go to the post office to pick up. It made her regret she had made the donation in the first place.

Sometimes people are reluctant to act because they are not sure what that action might lead to. If they write to a ministry about a spiritual need, will they receive a barrage of mail begging for donations? Unfortunately, such is often the case.

Maybe they will be embarrassed. I've been in services where the speaker asks those who would like to be prayed for just to "raise your hand." Then he asks all those who raised their hands to stand up. Finally, he asks them to come forward. If a person raises his hand and doesn't stand or come forward, someone approaches him and personally asks him to go forward. I find this method to be deceptive and intimidating. People will be less likely to take the first baby step of faith if they sense they may be pushed to go much further than they wish to.

Some people are quite shy. It is hard for them to take an action that requires some kind of performance in front of a large group. For example, some people find it very difficult to be baptized in front of the entire church. For these, perhaps we could have an informal baptismal service for just a few family members and friends.

Model the Action

Some things are easier "caught than taught." Demonstrate how to do the action you are suggesting or show a video or do a play. You could structure a group situation where one member models for another. For example, if you want members of your prayer group to more openly confess their weaknesses and sins, you could model the behavior by first confessing something. Another member would likely follow (after perhaps a little pause), then more would probably follow. Behavior tends to be contagious.

Model the behavior you want in others.

Have Receivers Mentally Rehearse the Behavior

For example, if you are teaching a class of high school students, you could discuss with them why they should say no to sex. You could ask the students if any of them have been in situations where they had to say no, and have them tell about it, if they are willing.

Then you could do a role-play or drama in which saying no in several situations is modeled. Then you could ask them to use their own imagination. You could say, "Close your eyes. Now, imagine you are at a party. There is music playing and a lot of people milling around. An attractive person of the opposite sex comes up to you and starts a conversation. Pretty soon he or she asks you if you would like to go upstairs. You know what that means. Think of how you would answer."

To the extent the students can make the mental rehearsal vivid and realistic they will remember it and be able to use it when the time comes. I'm helped in situations like this by a vivid memory. It actually happened while I was teaching at a secular university. I was working late on a hot summer night when a female student came to my office unexpectedly. She was very attractive, and provocatively dressed in a brief halter and shorts. She told me she "had to have me."

I was totally dumbfounded. Through God's grace I believe I did exactly the right thing. I didn't say a word. I knew I was attracted to her, and I felt any delay could be fatal. So, I just walked quickly out of my office to my car and drove straight home. I left so quickly I left my office unlocked, and her in it. If this kind of thing should ever happen again, I know just what to do! It's the purpose of mental rehearsal to create a workable scenario in the mind that one can call on in difficult situations.

Sustaining Action

Many of the actions we want to bring about need to happen on a repeated or continuing basis, not just once. Here are some ideas for promoting repeated action.

287

Reward the Desired Behavior

Both learning theories and experience suggest that behavior which produces a reward tends to be repeated. If the reward stops, the behavior will also eventually stop. The behavior does not have to be rewarded every time, but it must be rewarded at least some of the time.

What is a reward? It is something a person finds pleasurable, or it could be a way to avoid pain. A reward could be as simple as a kind word, or attention. It could be an insight, the solution to a problem. It could be a paycheck, or the satisfaction of having done a good job.

Reward behavior and it will more likely be repeated.

I would like to believe that I am sufficiently mature, self-directed, and purposeful; therefore, I don't need any extrinsic reward. I'm not. I get discouraged if I don't receive a kind word from time to time. I especially like it when alumni return and have good things to say about what they learned.

I remember how disappointed I was when I was awarded a cheap paper certificate for 10 years of service. It seemed to devalue my work. I was pleased, however, to receive an attractive clock to commemorate 15 years of service. Those who supervise others should not minimize the importance of such symbols.

Build a Habit

When I drive the 14 miles to work, I don't have to give much thought about how to get there. The habit of years is so ingrained that the car seems to drive itself. The same is true with my morning routine of shaving and bathing. On Sunday mornings my wife and I don't have to decide whether we are going to church. We are in the habit of going. We just go.

Good habits are helpful. We don't have to expend much thought on routine activities. In the same way, bad habits can be harmful because the behavior seems to take place automatically.

To build a good habit the behavior needs to be repeated several times. If, for example, you want someone to come regularly to a class, it won't necessarily be enough to get her there once. She may feel a bit awkward the first time there. Continue to reward and encourage the person to come back several times, until the behavior becomes habitual.

The Pleasure Principle

In one sense, human behavior isn't very complicated. We usually behave in a way that we believe will maximize our pleasure and minimize our pain.

Pleasure isn't a bad thing. If eating weren't enjoyable, some of us would get so busy we would forget to do it. If sex didn't give such pleasure, it would probably seem disgusting and the human race would have died out long ago. God designed us so that doing many of the things we need to do to sustain life give us pleasure.

Of course there needs to be balance and control. If one lives for the pleasure of eating, it can destroy him. Promiscuous sex spreads disease and brings children into the world under less than ideal circumstances. Drugs give a great sense of pleasure while they are destroying the person.

Seeking after pleasure, then, must be balanced. Sometimes we need to forego immediate pleasure to make future pleasure possible. If a farmer doesn't work the soil and plant the crop, there will be no harvest. Excessive drinking will bring a person to poverty and disease.

Give people pleasure when they do the behavior you are trying to encourage.

If we wish to see good behavior sustained, then the "doer" must receive some kind of satisfaction — pleasure — from doing it. For the spiritually mature, the thought of pleasing God may be enough. For those of us who are not yet that mature, we may benefit from more immediate pleasure. Here are some ways you can give pleasure or joy to someone.

- Make physical contact. Greet people with a firm handshake, or even a hug if that is appropriate.

- Remember people's names. People like to hear their names.

- Greet people warmly.

- Thank people promptly and appropriately for their service. The thanks should be as personal as possible. My wife and I just got a thank-you letter for a gift we gave to a Christian ministry. It was a fair-sized gift for us. In return we received an obvious form letter with the signature initialed by a secretary. It didn't make us feel very special.

  On the other hand, another organization we give to always sends a letter with a handwritten note from the president or a vice president. It makes us feel much appreciated.

- When you express appreciation, make it specific. Rather than saying something like, "I enjoyed your talk," say something like, "I appreciated your teaching on predestination. That's an area I didn't understand very well, and your lesson really helped."

- Recognize milestones. Many times steady progress goes almost unnoticed, but the accumulation becomes significant. You can keep track of wedding anniversaries, birthdays, anniversaries of the first day an employee started working for you, graduations, baptisms, and the like.

- Praise in public, correct in private. An employee complained to her boss that she never praised her. The boss was surprised. "I frequently tell you how much I appreciate your work. I told you just yesterday."

"Yes," said the employee, "but that doesn't count. You didn't do it in public."

Many people will find praise much more rewarding if it is done in public. Some, on the other hand, do not like a public display. Unless you have a reason to believe otherwise, err on the side of giving praise in public.

Correction, on the other hand, should be given in private. The idea is not to punish the person by public humiliation but to give information so problems can be avoided in the future.

■ Choose pleasant surroundings. Activities in attractive places are more rewarding than those in less appealing places. Some churches and classrooms have a dull, uninteresting look. Other places are exciting just to be in. Almost any activity will seem pleasant if it's held in a beautiful mountain or seashore setting.

■ Avoid irritations. Some things, such as sound, can become strongly negative if not done competently. If a place is so reverberant or noisy that people have to work hard to understand or be understood, that will create fatigue and an unpleasant association. Sound systems that are too loud, harsh, or distorted also are unpleasant.

Temperature, lighting, comfortable seating, appropriate "potty breaks," etc. are all things that need to be managed. While they won't necessarily make a positive impression if done right, they can leave a strong negative impression if done wrong.

■ Serve food. Almost any human situation can be made more pleasant by offering food and/or drink. It not only adds pleasure by meeting a physical need, but it often creates an atmosphere for informal interaction.

■ Watch the clock. People have limited attention spans. Remember, "the mind can only absorb what the seat can endure."

When I was a teenager I learned a principle about planning parties that has served me well. Always end each activity while people are still enjoying it. Don't wait until boredom begins to set in.

Respect people's time. Begin and end on time. Even if you begin late, end on time.

■ Express joy. Remember, "The joy of the LORD is your strength."⁶ Joy is contagious. Regardless of circumstances you can find joy. Most of the people I think of as joyful do not have less trouble in their lives than the rest of us — they just have a better attitude about it. James says to "consider it pure joy"⁷ when you face trials because you know these trials are making you more like Christ. If you are an upbeat, joyful person, it will be rewarding just to be with you!

The Limits of Persuasion

What makes followers of cult leaders such as Jim Jones, Charles Manson, or David Koresh willing to follow them even to death? There are many other examples, less extreme, where well-meaning people have been taken in and followed a leader who proved to be unworthy. Why?

We must acknowledge that there is significant power in the manipulation of words and symbols. People can sometimes be convinced that a lie is the truth. Both as followers and leaders we must guard against deception.

Recognize your limits.
Respect other people's God-given right to choose.

Here are some principles to consider to avoid following a cult leader, or acting like one!

- Leaders must be accountable to other human beings. A pastor should be accountable to the congregation, a board, or a church hierarchy. A ministry must have a board which has the real power and authority to fire or discipline the leader. Make sure the board is independent, that is, not made up of the leader's relatives and employees! If a leader claims he is accountable only to God, watch out!

  If anyone could claim to answer to God alone, it would have been the apostles through whom the church was established and the New Testament given. But even they were under the authority of others. Paul sharply corrected Peter about his hypocrisy in not eating with Gentiles.[8] And Paul put himself under the authority of the church at Jerusalem in settling a dispute.[9]

- Teachings must be in harmony with the Bible. Follow the example of the Bereans, who received Paul's teachings with enthusiasm and examined the Scriptures to see if they were true.[10]

  But it's not enough that the leader uses Scripture to defend his teaching. The devil quoted Scripture when tempting Jesus.[11] Even Charles Manson used Scripture. By lifting Scripture out of context, anyone can support a crazy idea. To avoid the drift into a cult, examine teachings on the basis of a good understanding of the entire thrust of Scripture, not just a few carefully selected words.

- The communication system should be open to various voices and views. Cults usually dominate or entirely control members' input. If a person is cut off from all other information, the teachings of the cult leader seem more reasonable. Cult leaders often isolate their followers from family and friends. They fill their lives so full of activities they have no time for anything else. In some cases followers are not allowed to talk with others. Some also use sleep deprivation or drugs to make their followers more suggestible.

Then what about a conference or a camp? Is it dangerous to isolate yourself for a few days at a Christian conference? The difference is, the camp or conference lasts only a few days, while a cult maintains "thought control" over long periods of time. I would be very suspicious of any group that attempts to control input to their members for long periods of time.

■ Know your ethical limits in communication. You and I are not responsible for anyone else's behavior, only our own. I must be obedient in presenting truth clearly, persuasively, accurately. But I am not authorized to use force or deception to cause others to accept and act on truth. Had God wanted to, He could have forced everyone to accept the truth. He chose not to. I must respect His choice, and the power of choice He has granted to my fellow human beings.

Chapter Summary

Action does not necessarily follow intention. Intentions may be forgotten, unrealistic, or may not take social realities into account. A person may not know how to accomplish the intention, or may just procrastinate until the intention is forgotten.

You will be more likely to get action if you ask for the action you want. The request should be for a specific action *now*. If the action cannot be performed immediately, you can ask for a commitment.

Getting people to take a small, immediate step toward a larger action is often useful. Through taking the initial step the person becomes more aware of his intention to do the action.

You will get more behavioral change if the actions you ask for are easy and non-threatening, and if you model the behavior. If the action is difficult or must be performed at a later time, have listeners mentally rehearse it.

Many times the action you want must be sustained, habitual. To get behavior to be repeated it should be rewarded. Anything that is pleasurable to the person will be rewarding. This would include a handshake or hug, a sincere thank-you, recognition or praise, pleasant surroundings, and food.

There are ethical limits to persuasion. Just as Jesus did, we must respect the humanity of others and not unfairly or unduly influence them.

1. For a summary of some of this literature, see Alexis S. Tan, *Mass Communication Theories and Research*, 2nd ed. (New York: John Wiley and Sons, 1985), 211–18.

2. See Romans 7:18-19.

3. See Romans 8:13.

4. See James 1:22-25.

5. For a discussion on when a "boomerang" effect may happen, see Thomas Nash *The Effectiveness of Interposing Time Intervals between Message Segments As a Means of Increasing Attitude Change among Highly Ego-involved Subjects*, unpublished doctoral dissertation (East Lansing: Michigan State University, 1976).

6. See Nehemiah 8:10.

7. See James 1:2.

8. See Galatians 2:11-14.

9. See Acts 15:1-21.

10. See Acts 17:11.

11. See Matthew 4:1-11.

Appendix A

The God Design Kit

by Tom Nash

Scene: Patent attorney's office. A person comes in with a large, paper bag marked "God Design Kit" in large letters. There is a sign on a counter or wall saying, "Patent Attorney." (If you want to involve more actors, you could have several people holding strangely shaped packages seated around a waiting room. Another inventor could be just leaving the counter as we begin.)

Jones: Next.

Smith: (APPROACHING DESK) I guess that's me.

Jones: OK. What you got?

Smith: A God Design Kit.

Jones: A what?

Smith: (SHOWS BAG LETTERING) A God Design Kit.

Jones: (Beat) What's it for . . . like primitive religions?

Smith: Oh no. Almost everybody these days designs their own god. Don't you?

Jones: Of course not. God . . . already exists.

Smith: Well, some people believe that. A few . . . eccentrics.

Jones: You think only eccentrics believe in God?

Smith: No. Almost everyone believes in God. That's why this kit is going to be a bestseller.

Jones: I don't get it. If people already believe in God . . . why would they . . . ??

Smith: That's just the point. People don't really believe

in a (EXAGGERATED AWE) God out there somewhere. You know, the scary kind. They prefer the more comfortable, manageable kind.

Jones: But . . . you can't just make a god.

Smith: No trouble at all. People do it all the time. Designer jeans, designer shoes, why not designer gods?

Jones: How would you go about it?

Smith: That's where this little kit comes in. It frees the imagination. Lets you create a much better god.

Jones: What have you got in there?

Smith: (TAKES OUT PACKAGE OF MODELING CLAY, THUMPS IT DOWN ON DESK) The most important part is the clay.

Jones: Modeling clay?

Smith: You see, that's the genius of this system. It's very flexible. Let's say you're into . . . body building. With just a little practice you can create a god with the (FLEXING MUSCLES) biggest pecs you've ever seen. Or let's say you're into sex . . . with just a little adjustment (MOTIONING TOWARD CHEST) you can . . .

Jones: I get the idea. So, if you're into . . . uh . . . cars, you make a car god.

Smith: Oh, yeah. I was into that for a while.

Jones: What if you're into . . . your family? You know, the wife, kids, dog, swimming pool. You know the scene.

Smith: It's kind of complicated, but after a while you get it. Cute, big-eyed little girls, tough little guys.

Jones: But, it's still just clay. It doesn't seem very permanent.

298

Smith: That's another great thing. You can change your god any time you want to.

Jones: Yea. (WISTFULLY) I don't know. I guess I always thought of God as being . . . bigger.

Smith: Nooo problem. (THUMPING ANOTHER PACKAGE OF CLAY ON THE DESK) You can always add more clay as needed. I know one guy who got his god really big . . . must have weighed 50 pounds. Cost him a fortune. 'Course I don't mind (CHUCKLES).

Jones: It's so . . . grey.

Smith: (PULLING OUT PAINTS) That's why we have paints. If you're into nature . . . just paint your god green. Or, how about a mellow-yellow god? Or maybe a red god to help you paint the town red.

Jones: You think this will sell?

Smith: Sell? I know it will. Look. Everybody's into designing their own god these days. Only most of them don't know how to do it. No imagination. When word of this kit gets out . . . they won't be able to keep them in the stores.

Jones: Yea. I'm afraid you may be right.

(CURTAIN DOWN, OR BLACKOUT, OR JONES SHOWS MR. SMITH OFF STAGE)